Speak Business English Like an American

Говорите на деловом английском как американцы!

Изучайте идиомы и выражения, незаменимые для успешной карьеры!

AMY GILLETT

LANGUAGE
SUCCESS
PRESS

ANN ARBOR, MICHIGAN

WITHDRAWN

First Edition

ISBN 0-9725300-7-X
Library of Congress Control Number: 2005907021

Translations by Larisa Keselman
Illustrations by Evgeny Kran

Visit our website: www.languagesuccesspress.com

Bulk discounts are available. For information, please contact:

Language Success Press
2232 S. Main Street #345
Ann Arbor, MI 48103
USA

E-mail: sales@languagesuccesspress.com
Fax: (303) 484-2004 (USA)

Printed in the United States of America

bells and whistles the name of the game ~~of both worlds~~ on top of trends through the roof on the same page nothing ~~...~~ pull out all the st~~...~~ ~~...~~ on the back cash cow step up to the plate dream up on the right track generate lots of buzz more bank for the buck wear many hats

СОДЕРЖАНИЕ

ПРЕДИСЛОВИЕ..1

LESSON 1:   Talking about a new project...................3

LESSON 2:   Talking about financial issues................9

LESSON 3:   Discussing a new ad campaign...............15

LESSON 4:   Talking about manufacturing..................21

LESSON 5:   Talking about company strategy.............27

REVIEW: LESSONS 1-5..32

LESSON 6:   Discussing good results........................35

LESSON 7:   Discussing bad results.........................41

LESSON 8:   Discussing a difficult decision...............47

LESSON 9:   Dealing with a dissatisfied customer.....53

LESSON 10: Discussing a difficult request................57

REVIEW: LESSONS 6-10......................................62

LESSON 11: Motivating co-workers..........................65

LESSON 12: Running a meeting................................71

LESSON 13: Discussing a mistake............................77

LESSON 14: Taking credit for good results................81

LESSON 15: Shifting blame.....................................87

REVIEW: LESSONS 11-15....................................92

LESSON 16: Politely disagreeing with someone......................95

LESSON 17: Telling somebody off...101

LESSON 18: Discussing office scandals...................................107

LESSON 19: Complaining about a co-worker.........................113

LESSON 20: Talking about a brown noser.............................117

REVIEW: LESSONS 16-20..124

LESSON 21: Explaining that you're feeling overworked........127

LESSON 22: Calling in sick...133

LESSON 23: Requesting a bank loan......................................137

LESSON 24: Negotiating a purchase......................................143

LESSON 25: Conducting a performance review....................149

REVIEW: LESSONS 21-25..153

LESSON 26: Promoting an employee......................................155

LESSON 27: Firing somebody..161

LESSON 28: Job interview 1..167

LESSON 29: Job interview 2..173

LESSON 30: Negotiating a salary offer..................................179

REVIEW: LESSONS 26-30..184

СЛОВАРЬ ТЕРМИНОВ..186

КЛЮЧИ К УПРАЖНЕНИЯМ..190

ИНДЕКС ИДИОМ...196

bells and whistles the name of the game track record the best of both worlds ... ds through the roof on the sa **ПРЕДИСЛОВИЕ** stake in the ground pull ... nutshell nothing to sneeze at a pat on the back cash cow step up to the plate

Хорошо это или плохо, но американская деловая речь буквально насквозь пронизана идиомами. Люди не просто начинают проект: they *get it off the ground.* Они не звонят друг другу с тем, чтобы обсудить его статус: they *touch base.* Позже, если с проектом что-то не ладится, его не закрывают: they *pull the plug.*

Книга «Speak Business English Like An American» включает в себя свыше 350 идиом и выражений, которые часто встречаются в деловой речи. Познакомьтесь с ними! Когда вы услышите их в разговоре с американцами, вы будете готовы дать уверенный ответ, а не молчать, терзаясь вопросом: чтобы бы это могло значить? Sales *went through the roof*? Какая еще крыша?.. Пока вы задаете себе подобные вопросы, беседа продолжается, но уже без вас. Увы, вы «выпали» из разговора: you're *out of the loop.*

После того, как вы ознакомитесь с идиомами, начните прислушиваться и старайтесь находить их в повседневных разговорах и в прессе. Идиомы – везде. Такие газеты, как *The Wall Street Journal* и бизнес-разделы других печатных изданий, полны идиом. Когда вы почувствуете, что понимаете их смысл, попробуйте употребить их в разговоре с друзьями и коллегами. Идиомы придадут живость вашей речи, сделают ее более колоритной!

Однако не пытайтесь «нагрузить» идиомами каждое предложение. Только к месту сказанная фраза будет иметь должный эффект: will *do the trick.*

Совсем не обязательно включать в свой лексикон абсолютно все идиомы, предложенные в этой книге. Подойдите избирательно к их использованию, отдав предпочтение наиболее, на ваш взгляд, полезным! Некоторые популярные идиомы, например, такие как *think outside the box* или *on the same page*, стали попросту «избитыми», но, даже если вы не будете их применять, их следует знать, так как, вероятнее всего, вам придется с ними столкнуться.

Происхождение американских идиом связано в основном с различными сферами человеческой деятельности. Многие идиомы деловой речи пришли из военного лексикона (например, *rally the troops*) и спорта (*step up to the plate*). Это свидетельствует о том, что американцы ассоциируют бизнес с состязаниями, где есть победители и побежденные. Подобно спорту, бизнес – это игра со своими правилами, где призы достаются тем командам (компаниям), которые превосходят остальных в стратегии и тактике.

Для вашего удобства все идиомы, используемые в этой книге, повторяются в разделе *Индекс идиом* в алфавитном порядке.

В разделе *Словарь терминов* объясняются значения многих других слов и выражений, с пониманием которых у вас могут возникнуть трудности. Если вам встречаются непонятные слова в диалогах урока и они набраны курсивом, вы можете тут же посмотреть их значение в конце книги.

Несомненно, полезными для вас окажутся практические упражнения, завершающие не только каждый урок, но и каждый тематический раздел. А *Ключи к упражнениям* подскажут, насколько хорошо вы овладели материалом.

К книге прилагается компакт-диск с записями всех диалогов. Он поможет вам уловить ритм и динамику американской речи и лучше запомнить идиомы. Используйте каждый удобный момент, чтобы лишний раз прослушать диалоги на CD – дома, на работе, в автомобиле, во время деловой поездки, – и, незаметно для себя, вы заговорите как настоящие американцы!

Желаем вам приятного путешествия в страну идиом! Надеемся, что оно будет для вас одновременно и увлекательным, и полезным, обогатит ваш язык и поможет вам в работе.

TALKING ABOUT A NEW PROJECT

Carl, Greg, and Anne work for WaterSonic Corporation. Recently, the company has come up with an idea for a new electric toothbrush.

Карл, Грэг и Энн работают в корпорации WaterSonic. Недавно компания выдвинула идею создания новой модели электрической зубной щетки.

Carl: I think we've **come up with a winner**.

Anne: I agree. The new Brush-o-matic toothbrush should be a **blockbuster**!

Carl: Our designers have already made up some *prototypes*.*
The toothbrushes have a tooth-whitening attachment and many other **bells and whistles**.

Greg: We should **fast track this project**. Let's try to *launch* it in time for the holiday season.

Anne: This will be a great **stocking stuffer**!

Carl: We definitely need a **big win** for the holidays.

Anne: This is a great idea. We're going to **make a killing**.

Greg: Let's not talk about this project to anybody who doesn't need to know. We'll **keep it under wraps**.

Carl: I agree. **Mum's the word**. We don't want any of our competitors to **get wind of** the idea and **rip it off**!

Anne: Right. Let's meet again on Monday morning and discuss our **game plan** for **getting this project off the ground**!

*Пояснения к выделенным курсивом словам и фразам см. на стр. 186-189.

IDIOMS & EXPRESSIONS – LESSON 1

(to) come up with a winner – to think up a very good idea
предложить удачную деловую идею, выигрышное решение

➤ Everybody likes Pepsi's new advertising campaign. Their advertising agency has **come up with a winner**.

blockbuster – a big success; a huge hit
настоящий успех; огромная популярность

➤ Eli Lilly made a lot of money with the prescription drug, Prozac. It was a real **blockbuster**.

Происхождение. Термин "blockbuster" вошел в лексикон королевских ВВС Великобритании как название особого вида бомб. Они отличались внушительными габаритами и огромной взрывной мощностью. Идеи, которые производят эффект взорвавшейся бомбы, по ассоциации называют "blockbuster". (К счастью, они не вызывают разрушений, подобно бомбам!)

bells and whistles – extra product features; product features which are attractive, but not essential for the product to function
дополнительные свойства товаров (с использованием новейших технологий); эти свойства, привлекательные для покупателя, не являются определяющими в эксплуатации продукта

➤ Our office just got a new copier with all the **bells and whistles**. I'll probably never learn how to use all of its features!

(to) fast track a project – to make a project a high priority; to speed up the time frame of a project
дать проекту «зеленую улицу»; отдать приоритет какому-либо направлению; работать над проектом в ускоренном темпе, чтобы выполнить работу в более сжатые сроки, досрочно

➤ Let's **fast track this project**. We've heard rumors that our competitors are developing similar products.

stocking stuffer – a small gift given at Christmas time
небольшой подарок на Рождество

➤ These new mini travel pillows will make great **stocking stuffers**!

Примечание. Это выражение связано с распространенной традицией: в канун Рождества дети вывешивают разукрашенные чулки, чтобы Санта Клаус, делая обход, набил их всевозможными подарками.

big win – a huge success; a successful product
огромный успех; удачный продукт; большая удача

➤ The drug company spent millions on research and development, hoping that one of their new products would be a **big win**.

(to) make a killing – to make a lot of money
заработать кучу денег

➤ Jane **made a killing** on her Google stock and retired at age 40.

SYNONYM: to make a fortune

(to) keep something under wraps – to keep something secret; to not let anybody know about a new project or plan
умалчивать о чем-либо; держать от всех в секрете новый проект или план

➤ I'm sorry I can't tell you anything about the project I'm working on. My boss told me to **keep it under wraps**.

Примечание. Слово "wraps" означает «обертка, плед, пелерина» – все, чем можно накрыть или обернуть. "Under wraps" – это то, что укрыто от взгляда или спрятано.

---

mum's the word – let's keep quiet about this; I agree not to tell anyone about this
никому ни слова; нем как рыба; давайте держать язык за зубами; я согласен никому об этом не рассказывать

➤ Please don't tell anybody about our new project. Remember: **mum's the word**!

Происхождение. Слово "mum" происходит от мычания «ммм». Это единственный звук, который можно издать при плотно сжатых губах. (Попробуйте произнести что-либо отличное от «ммм», когда губы плотно сжаты, и вы убедитесь, что это невозможно!)

(to) get wind of – to find out about something, often sensitive information
прослышать; проведать о чем-либо; почуять что-то

➤ When the restaurant owner **got wind of** the fact that one of his waiters was stealing money from the cash register, he was furious.

(to) rip off – to copy an idea; to steal
украсть замысел; содрать что-то; скопировать; ограбить

> Why doesn't the Donox Company ever think up any original ideas? All they ever do is **rip off** their competitors!

Примечание. "Rip off" может быть также и существительным. Пример: We were charged $10,000 for a small advertisement in the newspaper. What a **rip off**! (Нам выставили счет на 10 тыс. долларов за небольшое рекламное объявление в газете. Это просто грабеж!)

game plan – an action plan; a plan for how a project will proceed
план действий; план реализации проекта

> The software company's **game plan** is to expand its operations into China and India over the next year.

Происхождение. Это словосочетание пришло из мира спорта. В футболе "game plan" означает «стратегия на победу». (Имеется в виду американский, а не европейский футбол (soccer).

(to) get something off the ground – to get started on something, often a project
запустить; начать что-либо, часто проект

> We've been sitting around talking about this project for months. It's time to take action and **get it off the ground**!

✍ PRACTICE THE IDIOMS

Найдите наилучшую замену выделенным словам:

1) Did the company think of this new product idea themselves? **No, they ripped it off from an inventor.**
   a) No, they paid an inventor for the idea.
   b) No, they stole the idea from an inventor.
   c) No, the inventor agreed to sell it to them.

2) Jill is planning to quit her job at the end of September, but **mum's the word**.
   a) don't tell anybody
   b) don't tell her mother
   c) she may change her mind

3) Sony has **made a killing on** its popular PlayStation line.
   a) lost money on
   b) made a lot of money on
   c) decided to stop producing

4) After receiving a large loan from the bank, the company was finally able to **get its project off the ground**.
   a) get started on the project
   b) cancel the project
   c) borrow money

5) That new software company seems very disorganized. Do they have a **game plan**?
   a) a plan for closing down their business
   b) a plan for developing new games
   c) a plan for how they will proceed to grow their business

6) Some experts recommend that when you're interviewing for a new job, you **keep your current salary under wraps**.
   a) you should tell the interviewer what your current salary is
   b) you should say you're making more than you're really earning
   c) you should not say how much you're currently earning

7) Don's new cell phone has a video camera and all sorts of other **bells and whistles**.
   a) fancy features
   b) things that make loud ringing noises and whistle tones
   c) features typical in a low-priced product

8) When investors **got wind of** the fact that the pharmaceutical company's drug increased the risk of heart attacks, the company's stock price fell.
   a) hid
   b) discovered
   c) got fed up over

ANSWERS TO LESSON 1, p. 190

I did some back-of-the-envelope calculations.

TALKING ABOUT FINANCIAL ISSUES

Juan and Diane work in the finance department of Delicious Delights, a company that makes snack foods. Here, they're discussing the financial projections for a new product line.

Хуан и Диана работают в финансовом отделе компании Delicious Delights, которая выпускает снэки (холодные закуски). В данный момент они обсуждают финансовое планирование для новой линии продукции.

Juan: I'm really excited about the *launch* of our new line of fat-free Delicious Delight donuts.

Diane: Me too. But before we go any further, we'd better make sure this *product line* is going to be profitable.

Juan: I did some **back-of-the-envelope calculations**. Take a look.

Diane: I see you've estimated $2 million for the new equipment. Where did you get that *figure*?

Juan: That's an **educated guess** based on some equipment I bought last year.

Diane: You're going to need to *double-check* that. Using old estimates can get us **in hot water**.

Juan: No problem. I'll get on the phone with the manufacturer in Dallas and get a *price quote*.

Diane: Do you have a sense for *market demand*? We should get the *forecasts* from the marketing department before we **crunch the numbers**.

Juan: We don't have those yet. Mary from marketing said maybe we'd have them next week.

Diane: It just **blows my mind** when marketing people want us to **run numbers** and they don't bring us the information we need!

Juan: If we end up **in the red** on this project, it's going to be their **heads on the chopping block**, not ours. They're the ones with P&L* responsibility!

Diane: Our CFO* won't **give this project the green light** until he sees all the numbers. If it doesn't look like we'll make money or at least **break even**, he'll **pull the plug** on the project.

* P & L – "profit & loss" – прибыль и потери. В обязанности ответственных за "profit & loss" входит обеспечение прибыльности бизнеса. Они составляют "P & L Statement" – сводный финансовый отчет, или отчет о прибыли и потерях.
* CFO – "chief financial officer" – главный финансовый директор. Один из руководителей компании, отвечающий за финансовые вопросы.

IDIOMS & EXPRESSIONS – LESSON 2

back-of-the-envelope calculations – quick calculations; estimates using approximate numbers, instead of exact numbers
быстрый подсчет; предварительные расчеты на базе приблизительных цифр вместо точных

➤ I don't need the exact numbers right now. Just give me some **back-of-the-envelope calculations**.

Примечание. Это выражение означает быстрые подсчеты, которые обычно делаются на любой бумаге под рукой, в том числе на обратной стороне какого-нибудь конверта.

educated guess – a guess based on experience; a piece of information based on prior knowledge, not hard facts or data
догадка на базе прежнего опыта; информация, основанная на имеющихся знаниях, а не на неопровержимых фактах

➤ I'd say there are about a million potential consumers for your new line of cosmetics, but that's just an **educated guess**.

10

in hot water – in trouble
в трудном положении

> Ian was **in hot water** with the government after he was caught making illegal copies of software.

(to) crunch the numbers – to perform financial calculations
производить финансовые подсчеты

> Reed Corporation is thinking about buying a small company. First, they'll need to **crunch the numbers** and see if their acquisition will be profitable.

Примечание. Вы можете встретить существительное, производное от этого выражения: «number cruncher» – бухгалтер, финансовый работник, который постоянно имеет дело с цифрами, производит сложные финансовые расчеты.

(it or that) blows my mind – it bothers me; it really surprises me; it amazes me
это меня беспокоит; это меня по-настоящему удивляет; это поражает мое воображение

> **It blows my mind that** our company is trying to save money by taking away our free coffee service.

(to) run (the) numbers – to perform financial calculations
производить финансовые расчеты, подсчитывать

> Should we lease or buy the equipment? We'll need to **run the numbers** to help us make the decision.

in the red – losing money; when expenses are more than revenues
нести убытки; когда расходы превышают доходы

> We need to do something to start making profits. If we're **in the red** for one more quarter, we're going to go out of business.

Примечание. Это выражение пришло из бухгалтерской практики отмечать дебиты (вычеты со счета) красным карандашом, кредиты (поступления на счет) – черным. Так выражение "in the black" является антонимом "in the red" и означает «получать прибыль».

one's head is on the chopping block – in a position where one is likely to be fired or get in trouble
попасть в беду; оказаться в ситуации, когда вам грозит увольнение или крупные неприятности

➤ After Earthy Foods released a frozen dinner that made many consumers sick, their CEO's **head was on the chopping block**.

Примечание. A "chopping block" – это чурбан, на котором рубят дрова или мясники разделывают туши. Человек, держащий голову на "chopping block", имеет шанс с ней расстаться. К счастью, не в прямом смысле: можно потерять работу, но не лишиться головы!

(to) give somebody the green light – to give permission to move forward with a project
дать добро на проект; дать кому-либо «зеленую улицу»

➤ Super Software's Moscow office has developed its own regional advertising campaign. They hope that headquarters in California will **give them the green light** to proceed with the campaign.

(to) break even – to make neither a profit or a loss; the point at which revenues equal costs
стать безубыточным, т. е. не получить прибыли, но и не остаться в убытке; достичь уровня, когда доходы равны расходам

➤ You **broke even** during your first year in business? That's good since most companies lose money during their first year.

(to) pull the plug – to put a stop to a project or initiative, usually because it's not going well
приостановить проект или инициативу, обычно из-за их бесперспективности; прекратить что-либо (финансирование), прервать

➤ After 10 years of drilling for oil in Nebraska and finding nothing, the oil company finally **pulled the plug** on its exploration project.

Происхождение. Это выражение часто ассоциируется с отключением от электропитания. Что происходит, когда вы вытаскиваете вилку из электрической розетки? Электроприбор перестает работать. В 19 веке, когда возник этот термин, слово "the plug" обозначало «затычку» для бочка в туалете. Чтобы спустить воду в туалете, надо было вытащить затычку из бочка.

✎ PRACTICE THE IDIOMS

Выберите наиболее подходящий ответ к каждому предложению:

1) Did our CEO give the green light for the new project yet?
   a) No, he told us he needed more information before making a decision.
   b) Yes, he told us that the project was a bad idea and that we should stop working on it.
   c) Yes, he's going to discuss the project with his wife and see what she thinks.

2) Last year, our company made a loss on our new line of video games, but this year we'll break even.
   a) I'm sorry to hear you're broke.
   b) That's great. At least you're making progress.
   c) Too bad. Last year you did a lot better.

3) If you don't double-check those numbers and make sure they're correct, you might get in hot water with your boss.
   a) You're right. My boss always appreciates it when I give him the wrong numbers.
   b) That would be great. My boss enjoys soaking in hot water.
   c) You're right. My boss always gets angry when he finds mistakes.

4) Our company is in the red again this quarter.
   a) Congratulations! When's the celebration party?
   b) In the red again? I hope you don't go out of business!
   c) In the red? That's okay. It's better than being in the black.

5) We should pull the plug on our online advertising campaign.
   a) I agree. It's not bringing us any new business.
   b) I agree. Let's double our spending on it.
   c) I disagree. I think we should stop spending money on online advertising.

6) I know our company is looking for ways to cut costs. Do you think my head is on the chopping block?
   a) No, don't worry. They won't fire you.
   b) No, I don't think so. But you might get fired.
   c) No, I don't think they'll cut off your head.

7) Doesn't it blow your mind that they promoted Beth to General Manager after the mess she made in our department?
   a) Yes, she really deserved that promotion.
   b) No, but it does surprise me.
   c) Yes, it really surprises me!

8) Did you have a chance to crunch those numbers yet?
   a) Yes, I put them in a blender and crunched them up.
   b) Yes, I just put the financial reports on your desk.
   c) Yes, I'll take a look at them next week.

ANSWERS TO LESSON 2, p. 190

DISCUSSING A NEW AD CAMPAIGN

Ted works for an advertising agency. He's presenting to Sam and Lisa, who work for Pacific Beer Company.

Тэд работает в рекламном агентстве. Он делает презентацию для Сэма и Лизы, которые работают в компании Pacific Beer.

Lisa: Ted would like to **run some ideas by us** for our new *ad campaign*.

Ted: Please **keep an open mind**. Remember that **nothing is set in stone** yet. We're still just **brainstorming**.

Sam: I hope that doesn't mean we're about to hear a lot of **half-baked ideas**!

Ted: I think you're going to like this. Our idea is to use a black bear as our *mascot*. Our **tagline** can be: "Strong enough to satisfy a bear."

Lisa: It would be great if people would *associate our brand with* a bear — strong and independent. That would really improve our *brand equity*.

Sam: I don't want to **throw cold water over** your idea, but where did you get the idea for a bear?

Ted: Didn't you hear about that bear at the campground a couple weeks ago? He entered a tent and drank two dozen Pacific beers! What a great *endorsement* for Pacific beer!

Lisa: I think we're **on the right track** with this campaign. The bear should **generate lots of buzz**. Everybody will be talking about the bear who loves Pacific beer!

Ted: And here's the **icing on the cake**: he won't demand **an arm and a leg** to **plug our product**. In fact, we can probably pay him in beer!

Sam: Okay, you've **twisted my arm**. Let's **run with the idea**.

Ted: Great. I'll **flesh it out** some more and **touch base with** you in a couple of days.

IDIOMS & EXPRESSIONS – LESSON 3

(to) run some ideas by someone – to discuss some new ideas
обсудить новые идеи, концепции с кем-либо

➤ Our R&D department has some ideas about how to make our products safer. They'd like to meet this afternoon to **run some ideas by us**.

Примечание. Вам также может встретиться это выражение в форме ед. числа: run an idea by someone

(to) keep an open mind – to be ready to accept new ideas; to not be biased
быть открытым к восприятию новых идей; быть беспристрастным, не иметь предубеждений

➤ Cathy's new boss starts next week. She's heard he's very difficult to work with, but she's trying to **keep an open mind**.

nothing is set in stone – nothing is decided yet; things can still be changed
еще ничего не решено окончательно; все еще можно изменить; на свете нет абсолютных истин; все течет, все изменяется

➤ If you don't like the new product design, we can still change it. **Nothing is set in stone** yet.

(to) brainstorm – to think up new ideas; to generate new ideas in a group
придумывать что-то новое; генерировать новые идеи сообща

➤ When the company started losing market share, the president called a meeting to **brainstorm** ways to turn around the business.

Примечание. Существует выражение "brainstorming session", когда группа людей собирается вместе, чтобы методом «мозговой атаки» выработать решение проблемы, обсудить новые идеи.

half-baked idea – a stupid or impractical idea or suggestion
«сырая», незрелая, непродуманная, бестолковая, бесполезная, неосуществимая идея или предложение

➤ I can't believe we paid that consulting company so much money. We wanted them to help us grow our business and all they did was give us a bunch of **half-baked ideas**!

(to) throw cold water over (an idea, a plan) – to present reasons why something will not work; to discourage
окатить ушатом холодной воды; представить серьезные аргументы, критические замечания; отбить охоту заниматься чем-либо

➤ Pat presented her boss with a plan to expand their business into China, but he **threw cold water on** her plan and told her to just focus on developing business in the United States.

Примечание. Встречается также вариант – to throw cold water on.

on the right track – proceeding in a good way; going in the right direction
идти верной дорогой; двигаться в правильном направлении

➤ After years of struggling, Apple Computer is now **on the right track** by focusing on innovative products like the iPod.

(to) generate lots of buzz – to cause many people to start talking about a product or service, usually in a positive way that helps to sell the product or service
заставить говорить о себе (продукции или услугах), обычно в положительном плане; привлечь всеобщее внимание; вызвать ажиотаж

➤ Procter & Gamble **generated lots of buzz** for its new toothpaste by giving away free samples to people on the streets of New York City.

Примечание. "Buzz" – популярное слово, употребляемое часто в значении «внимание».

icing on the cake – an additional advantage; when one good thing happens, then another good thing happens along with it
дополнительная выгода; когда все удачно складывается одно к другому

➤ Alison won $2 million in a sexual harassment lawsuit against her employer. And here's the **icing on the cake**: her company will have to pay all of her legal fees too!

Примечание. "Icing on cake" буквально означает «сахарная глазурь на торте», которую обычно используют в качестве украшения. Торт может быть и без нее достаточно вкусным, однако сахарная глазурь делает его еще аппетитнее.

---

an arm and a leg – a lot of money
втридорога; целое состояние

➤ William always flies business class to Asia. The plane tickets cost **an arm and a leg**!

(to) plug (a product) – to promote a product; to talk positively about a product
активно рекламировать товар; заниматься продвижением товара на рынке; «раскручивать» продукт; давать положительную оценку продукту

➤ American Express often hires famous people to **plug their credit cards**. No wonder people pay attention to their ads!

(to) twist somebody's arm – to convince somebody; to talk somebody into doing something
убедить кого-либо в чем-то; уговорить сделать что-либо

➤ Ben didn't want to go to the company Christmas party this year, but Amy **twisted his arm** and he ended up having fun.

(to) run with an idea – to proceed with an idea
приступить к воплощению идеи, начать реализацию проекта

➤ After much discussion, the language school decided to **run with the idea** of offering a free class to each potential client.

(to) flesh out something – to elaborate on something; to add more detail to a plan; to think in more detail about something

тщательно разработать, конкретизировать что-то; облекать плотью; продумать что-либо в деталях

> I like your idea of moving our manufacturing facility to China, but your plan doesn't have any details. Please **flesh out** your plan and present it at our board meeting next month.

(to) touch base with someone – to get in contact with; to make brief contact with

связаться с кем-либо; вступить в непродолжительный контакт

> "Hi, it's Andy calling from *City Style* magazine. I'm just **touching base with** you to see if you want to buy an ad."

tagline – a slogan; a phrase used to promote a product

лозунг – ключевая фраза, используемая для рекламного продвижения товара

> Meow Mix, a brand of cat food, has one of the best **taglines** in history: "Tastes so good, cats ask for it by name."

✎ PRACTICE THE IDIOMS

Найдите наилучшую замену выделенным словам:

1) Starting a chain of coffee houses in Manhattan is **a half-baked idea**! There are already more than enough coffee houses in Manhattan.
   a) a great idea
   b) a really bad idea
   c) an idea that needs some more time in the oven

2) The government is discussing a new proposal to raise the minimum wage, but **nothing is set in stone yet**.
   a) nothing has been decided yet
   b) the proposal has been approved
   c) nothing will ever be decided

3) You don't have to **twist the boss's arm**. She's already decided to let everybody leave early on Friday to avoid holiday traffic.
   a) convince the boss
   b) hurt the boss
   c) ignore the boss

4) Arnold Schwarzenegger has appeared on television commercials in Japan, China, Austria, and Brazil, **plugging products** such as vitamin drinks and soup.
   a) drinking products
   b) advertising products
   c) terminating products

5) Before approaching a bank for a loan, you need to **flesh out** your business plan.
   a) throw out
   b) present
   c) add more detail to

6) Buying a new computer system would cost **an arm and a leg**. Let's just upgrade the system we already have.
   a) a lot of money
   b) not much money
   c) a lot of time

7) Paul and Susan make a good living running a bed-and-breakfast in Vermont. Meeting lots of friendly people is **the icing on the cake**.
   a) easy when you live in Vermont
   b) how they earn their living
   c) an additional benefit

8) I like your idea of selling our products by direct mail. **Let's run with it.**
   a) Let's discuss it further.
   b) Let's proceed with it.
   c) Let's forget it.

ANSWERS TO LESSON 3, p. 190

Lesson 4

TALKING ABOUT MANUFACTURING

Mike and Dan work for Swift Shoes, a manufacturer of sneakers. Mike is in charge of manufacturing. Dan is trying to push Mike to get some new shoes ready quickly.

Майк и Дэн работают в компании Swift Shoes, выпускающей кроссовки. Майк отвечает за производство. Дэн пытается подтолкнуть Майка к ускоренному внедрению в производство новых моделей обуви.

Dan: We've decided to launch our new spring shoe on April 20th.

Mike: We're still trying to **work out the kinks** in our manufacturing process. Our factory is China is having trouble with the soles.

Dan: I know that, Mike. But you've still got three months. It should be plenty of time.

Mike: It could take another six months to **fine-tune** our manufacturing process.

Dan: Well, we don't have that much time. **No ifs, ands, or buts**, we need to launch on April 20th.

Mike: **Just for the record**, I think we're **cutting it a little close**. I recommend we launch on July 20th instead.

Dan: We can't. We've already decided on the **tagline**: "Spring into spring with Swift's new spring shoe."

Mike: It's time for a **reality check**. I'm telling you we might not be ready by April 20th, and you're telling me we have to be because of a **tagline**?

21

Dan: Mike, now's the time to **step up to the plate** and **get the job done**.

Mike: Well, I'm going to be working **down to the wire**.

Dan: Just **do whatever it takes**. Just make sure we've got a million pairs of shoes in *inventory* by the April 20th deadline.

Mike: I'm going to have to run the factories **24/7**. That's going to be a lot of *overtime pay*.

Dan: **At the end of the day**, a little extra expense doesn't matter. We just want those shoes ready by April 20th.

IDIOMS & EXPRESSIONS – LESSON 4

(to) work out the (or some) kinks – to solve the problems with
найти решение проблем; распутать узел проблем

➤ The company announced that they will delay the launch of their new product by two weeks. They still need to **work out the kinks** with their packaging process.

Примечание. A "kink" – это недоработка или упущение (ошибка) в системе или плане

(to) fine-tune – to make small adjustments to something to increase the effectiveness or to make something work better
настроить, наладить, отрегулировать что-либо; произвести небольшие доработки для повышения эффективности; привести что-либо в действие

➤ Rick hired an executive coach to help him **fine-tune** his managerial skills.

no ifs, ands, or buts – no excuses; it's absolutely necessary that; this is how it's going to be no matter what anybody says
никаких «но»; никаких «если»; никаких возражений или оправданий; это абсолютно необходимо; вот как это должно быть, невзирая на чьи-либо разговоры

➤ All employees must attend our team-building workshop tomorrow, **no ifs, ands, or buts**.

just for the record (also: for the record) – let me make my opinion clear

примите к сведению; разрешите мне разъяснить свою позицию; официально высказать свою точку зрения

➤ I know that everybody else likes the idea of using a bear for a mascot, but, **just for the record**, I think it's a lousy idea.

(to) cut it (a little) close – to try to do too much before a deadline; to not leave enough time to get a task done

пытаться сделать слишком много за очень короткий срок; когда времени в обрез для завершения работы

➤ Jerry promised his customer he'd ship out the farm equipment by the end of the week. Since we haven't assembled it yet, I think that's **cutting it close**.

---

tagline – *see Lesson 3*

---

reality check – let's think realistically about this situation (said when you don't like something that's being suggested because you don't think the other person is thinking practically or logically)

давайте здраво оценим ситуацию (так говорится, когда вам не нравится чье-то предложение, так как вы не считаете, что этот человек рассуждает реалистично или логически)

➤ You think we can start selling our products through our website next month? Time for a **reality check**! Nobody at our company knows anything about e-commerce.

(to) step up to the plate – to take action; to do one's best; to volunteer

начать действовать; стараться изо всех сил; добровольно соглашаться на что-либо

➤ We need somebody to be in charge of organizing the company holiday party. Who'd like to **step up to the plate** and start working on this project?

Примечание. Игрок наступает на базу (plate), когда приходит его очерь бить по мячу.

(to) get the job done – to do the job successfully; to accomplish the task
успешно завершить работу; довести дело до конца

➤ We plan to outsource all of our software development to IBM. We know they have the resources to **get the job done**.

(to) work down to the wire – to work until the last minute; to work until just before the deadline
работать до упора; полностью выкладываться; работать до последнего

➤ The investment bankers need to turn in their report at 9 a.m. tomorrow morning, and they've still got many hours of work left on it. They're going to be working **down to the wire**.

Примечание. Это выражение связано с лошадиными бегами. В 19 веке на американских ипподромах над финишной чертой беговых дорожек был натянут провод. Это помогало определить, какая лошадь первой пересекала финишную прямую. В гонке "down to the wire" было довольно сложно определить победителя до последней секунды.

(to) do whatever it takes – to do anything and everything necessary to accomplish a task or reach a goal
делать все возможное и невозможное для достижения поставленной цели

➤ It's very important that our new product be ready before Christmas. **Do whatever it takes** to make that happen.

24/7 – around the clock; 24 hours a day, 7 days a week
круглосуточно; 24 часа в сутки, 7 дней в неделю

➤ During tax season, many accountants work **24/7**.

at the end of the day – in summary; when we look back on this after we're finished
в конечном счете; в результате; в итоге; когда мы оглядываемся назад после завершения работы над чем-либо

➤ **At the end of the day**, the most important thing is how many cases of product we were able to ship this year.

✎ PRACTICE THE IDIOMS

Заполните пропуски, используя следующие идиомы:

working down to the wire
get the job done
cutting it close
24/7
reality check
fine-tuning
work out the kinks
does whatever it takes

Tom is a plant manager at Chocolate Delights, a manufacturer of chocolate. To prepare for the holiday season, the chocolate factory operates _____(1)_____ and doesn't shut down for even an hour. Tom is very hardworking and every year _____(2)_____ to get a large amount of chocolate produced to meet the holiday demand. This year, Chocolate Delights decided to make a new type of chocolate Santa Claus. There were some problems with the manufacturing process, but Tom was able to _____(3)_____. It was just a matter of _____(4)_____ one of the machines. Tom's goal is to have 100,000 boxes of chocolate ready to ship by November 1. Will he reach this goal? Probably, but he'll be _____(5)_____. Nancy, Tom's boss, is afraid he's _____(6)_____ this year. "Time for a _____(7)_____," she told him this morning. "If you don't speed up production, you're not going to reach your quota." Tom just smiled and replied, "Don't worry, I'll _____(8)_____. You can count on me."

ANSWERS TO LESSON 4, p. 190

Our latest model cell phone was a real dog.

TALKING ABOUT COMPANY STRATEGY

Andy and Laura work for Saltonica, a maker of cell phones. Sales have been slow lately, so Andy is recommending the company adopt a new strategy.

Энди и Лора работают в фирме Saltonica, выпускающей сотовые телефоны. В связи с тем, что в последнее время наблюдается заметный спад продаж, Энди считает, что компания должна перейти на новую стратегию.

Andy: My team has come up with a new strategy. We can't continue being **fast followers**. We need to start developing our own **cutting-edge** technologies.

Laura: Why? We've been **fast followers** for the past ten years. **Why mess with success?**

Andy: Success? **Get with the program**. Our sales are way down. Our **cash cow**, the Model 8B, only sold 900 units last month!

Laura: I can understand why. That phone's a *relic*. It's been around for over three years. What about our new phones?

Andy: Our latest model cell phone was a **real dog**! It sold only 20 percent of our sales *forecast*.

Laura: Any idea why?

Andy: *Product life cycles* are much shorter now than before. New technologies are developed at a much faster rate.

Laura: So what are we supposed to do?

Andy: We need to become much more *innovative* as a company. Instead of producing **me-too products**, we need to **leapfrog our competitors**.

Laura: How do we do that?

Andy: **For starters**, we need to **beef up** our *R&D* department. We need to develop *differentiated products* which we can sell **at a premium**.

Laura: As a next step, let's **get buy-in** from our marketing and sales directors.

Andy: Right. We should get everyone **on the same page**.

IDIOMS & EXPRESSIONS – LESSON 5

fast followers – a company that doesn't come up with new ideas or concepts first, but rather quickly copies those of other companies
ловкие имитаторы; компания, которая не предлагает новые идеи, но быстро копирует новшества других фирм; досл.: быстрые последователи

➤ Taiwanese PC manufacturers don't spend much on R&D. They are **fast followers**, waiting for foreign competitors to innovate and then quickly copying their products.

cutting-edge – very modern; using the latest technologies
самый современный и передовой; использующий новейшие технологии

➤ Sony focuses on innovation and is known for its **cutting-edge** electronic goods.

Why mess with success? – Why start doing things differently when the way we're doing them now has been working?
Зачем менять ход вещей, когда все и так прекрасно работает? От добра добра не ищут!

➤ We could move our manufacturing plant to China, but we're doing well manufacturing in the United States. **Why mess with success?**

(to) get with the program – to pay attention to what's going on right now; to be alert to what's happening now
обращать внимание на то, что происходит в данный момент; следить за текущими событиями

➤ **Get with the program**. Our competitors have all started to outsource their call centers to India to save money, while we're still paying a fortune here in the United States!

cash cow – a product, service, or business division that generates a lot of cash for the company, without requiring much investment
товары, услуги или подразделения в бизнесе, приносящие компании хороший доход и не требующие при этом солидных капиталовложений; «дойная корова»

➤ With strong sales every year and a great brand name, Mercedes is a **cash cow** for DaimlerChrysler.

real dog – an unsuccessful product; a commercial failure
коммерческая неудача

➤ In 1985, the Coca-Cola Company released New Coke. It was a **real dog** and was in stores for only a few months.

me-too products – products that are extremely similar to another company's products; imitations
товары, которые как две капли воды похожи на продукцию другой компании; имитации

➤ Procter & Gamble is a company famous for innovation. They rarely produce **me-too products**.

(to) leapfrog one's competitors – to make a product that is technologically superior to competitors' products
обскакать конкурентов; выпустить продукт, который в технологическом плане на голову выше продукции конкурентов

➤ Logitech introduced a product that **leapfrogged its competitors**: a mouse that was both wireless and *ergonomic*.

Примечание. "Leapfrog" – чехарда, популярная детская игра, когда один играющий нагибается, а другой перепрыгивает через его спину.

for starters – as a first step; to begin with
для начала; сначала

> You want to do business in India? **For starters**, I'd recommend setting up an office in Mumbai.

(to) beef up – to improve; to add to
улучшить; усовершенствовать; добавить что-либо

> Leave plenty of extra time at the airport. Ever since they **beefed up** security, it takes a long time to get through the lines.

at a premium – at a high price; at a relatively high price
выше номинала; по сравнительно высокой цене

> When flat-screen televisions first came out, they were selling **at a premium.**

(to) get buy-in (from) – to get agreement or approval from
получить согласие или одобрение

> To be an effective leader, you need to **get buy-in** for your decisions from employees throughout the organization.

(to be) on the same page – to be in agreement; when everybody has the latest information on what's going on
действовать согласованно; когда все в равной мере располагают последней информацией

> Before we start on the next phase of this project, let's have a meeting and make sure everybody's **on the same page.**

Примечание. В последнее время это выражение используется настолько часто, что потеряло свою выразительность и перешло в разряд штампов. Вам важно знать его значение, однако не следует злоупотреблять им в разговоре.

✎ PRACTICE THE IDIOMS

Найдите наилучшую замену выделенным выражениям:

1) Mattel, a large toy company, always **beefs up** its advertising around the holiday season.
   a) changes
   b) increases
   c) decreases

30

2) Amazon.com uses **cutting-edge** technologies to determine which products each of its customers is most likely to buy.
   a) sharp
   b) inexpensive
   c) the most modern

3) We need to re-design our store. **For starters**, we should move the cash register from the back of the store to the front of the store.
   a) as a final step
   b) as a first priority
   c) for people who can't find the cash register now

4) Your company is introducing garlic fruitcake? **That sounds like a real dog!**
   a) What a great idea!
   b) That sounds like a terrible idea!
   c) I'm sure dogs will love it!

5) After Apple's iPod proved to be successful, several other manufacturers came out with **me-too products**.
   a) products very similar to the iPod
   b) their own innovative products
   c) products very different from the iPod

6) Your plan is good, but before you proceed, you'll need to **get buy-in** from the company president.
   a) get a purchase order
   b) get approval
   c) get a promotion

7) With our new solar-powered automobile, we're going to **leapfrog our competitors**.
   a) make all our competition disappear
   b) turn our competitors into small green animals
   c) come out with a superior product

8) You don't own a cell phone? I thought everybody had one. You need **to get with the program**!
   a) get a program to teach you how to use the phone
   b) join a cell phone calling plan that offers unlimited minutes
   c) get a cell phone too so you're not missing what everybody else has

ANSWERS TO LESSON 5, p. 190

REVIEW FOR LESSONS 1-5

Вставьте пропущенные слова:

1) Steve won't be satisfied with a simple digital camera. He wants one with all the _____ and whistles.

   a) widgets   b) bells   c) chimes

2) I know you're planning on spending your entire advertising budget on TV advertising. _____ for the record, I don't think that's a good idea.

   a) just   b) only   c) simply

3) HBO _____ up with a winner with its popular show *Sex and the City*. It became an international hit.

   a) came   b) thought   c) arrived

4) Jack didn't want to buy laptops for everybody in the office, but the office manager succeeded in twisting his _____ .

   a) leg   b) mind   c) arm

5) After two years on the market, this product is still not selling well. I think we should _____ the plug.

   a) push   b) remove   c) pull

6) Our president has made it very clear that we need to double our revenues this year. No _____, ands, or buts.

   a) ifs   b) howevers   c) maybes

7) We don't have any job openings right now, but please _____ base with us in a couple of months.

   a) reach   b) contact   c) touch

8) Irene would like to start a business from her home, but she's not sure how to go _____ it.

    a) around   b) about   c) with

9) Some of your colleagues might not like you, but at the _____ of the day, what really matters is what your boss thinks of you.

    a) end   b) close   c) finish

10) When it was clear that the new product was a failure, nobody was willing to step up to the _____ and take responsibility.

    a) table   b) plate   c) dish

11) Holiday time is very busy at the department store, so the store is planning on beefing _____ its sales staff for the entire month of December.

    a) out   b) over   c) up

12) Charlie loves his job, so when he won the employee of the year award, it was just _____ on the cake.

    a) frosting   b) icing   c) candles

13) Don't tell Tony we're planning a retirement party for him. It's going to be a surprise. _____ the word!

    a) Sister's   b) Dad's   c) Mum's

14) After another bad quarter, the president's head was on the _____.

    a) cutting board   b) chopping block   c) operating table

15) General Electric is thinking about selling off one of its businesses in India, but nothing is set in _____ yet.

    a) stone   b) rock   c) paper

ANSWERS TO REVIEW, p. 191

Kudos to Linda!

DISCUSSING GOOD RESULTS

Peter, Linda, and Todd work as managers at Capital City Bank, a retail bank. Linda's creative idea for attracting new customers to the bank has generated lots of new business.

Питер, Линда и Тод работают менеджерами в Capital City Bank, банке, специализирующемся на обслуживании частных вкладчиков. Линдина оригинальная идея о том, как привлечь новых клиентов, дала хороший толчок бизнесу.

Peter: Great news! We had a **record-breaking** quarter. We brought in revenues of $500,000.

Linda: Wow, revenues really were **though the roof!**

Todd: That's great. **Kudos to** Linda! She deserves a **pat on the back**. The **guerrilla marketing** campaign she **dreamed up** was brilliant. She sent out e-mail to all of our customers asking them to e-mail a friend about our services. For each friend they e-mailed, they received a free gift.

Peter: Linda, your campaign helped us **drum up a lot of business**. We **signed on 800 new customers**.

Linda: I'm really glad my plan **panned out**. I thought it would, since everybody loves a *freebie!*

Todd: Linda, we can always count on you to **think outside the box**.

Linda: **For the record**, Peter helped me come up with the idea.

Peter: Thanks for **sharing the credit**, Linda. But it was your idea.

Todd: The important thing is that we're now **giving our biggest competitor, US Bank, a run for their money**.

record-breaking – better than ever before; exceeding previous results
побивший рекорды; превзошедший прежние результаты; достигший самых высоких показателей

➤ After another **record-breaking** quarter, eBay's stock price hit a new high.

(to be or to go) though the roof – to be or to go very high; to be or to go higher than expected
сильно подскочить; гораздо выше, чем ожидалось

➤ No wonder people are complaining about the cost of heating their homes. Oil prices have gone **through the roof**!

kudos to – I'd like to give credit to; I'd like to acknowledge
честь и хвала (кому-то); слава, почет, всеобщее признание и уважение; восхвалять, превозносить кого-то

➤ **Kudos to** our R&D department. They've come up with a new, improved shampoo formula that's also cheaper to manufacture.

a pat on the back – credit; recognition; praise
поддержка; признание; выразить одобрение; оказать поддержку; досл.: одобрительно похлопать кого-либо по спине

➤ "Team, give yourselves **a pat on the back**. Our results are in and we just had our most successful quarter ever!"

guerrilla marketing – innovative methods to sell products; non-traditional methods of advertising or promotion that deliver good results with minimal spending
использовать новаторские методы продажи товаров; нетрадиционные виды рекламного продвижения, приносящие позитивные результаты при минимальных затратах

➤ To promote his new Internet dating service, Don painted his car pink and wrote "Don's Dating Service" in big letters on both sides of the car. That's effective **guerrilla marketing**!

Примечание. "Guerrilla war" означает ведение партизанской войны при помощи независимых военных группировок, которые зачастую используют агрессивную и нетрадиционную тактику, чтобы одержать победу в бою.

dream up – to think up something creative or unusual; to come up with an original idea; to invent
проявить творческую фантазию; придумать что-либо неординарное; выдвинуть оригинальную идею

➤ A disposable lemon-scented toilet brush? What will companies **dream up** next?

(to) drum up business – to create business; to find new customers
вести коммерческую деятельность; создать бизнес; найти новых клиентов

➤ Sales have been very slow lately. Do you have any ideas for **drumming up business**?

(to) sign on new customers (or members) – to enlist new customers; to get customers to open an account or take a membership
зарегистрировать новых клиентов; подписать контракт; открыть для клиентов счет или членство

➤ The fitness center was able to **sign on 300 new members** in May thanks to their successful advertising campaign.

(to) pan out – to succeed; to bring the desired results
преуспеть в чем-либо; принести желаемые результаты

➤ When Steve's career in acting didn't **pan out**, he decided to go to business school.

(to) think outside the box – to think creatively; to think in a new and different way
проявлять творческий подход к делу; мыслить по-новому, нестандартно

➤ We're losing business. Let's **think outside the box** and come up with some creative ways to market our services.

Происхождение. Это выражение имеет отношение к ребусу-головоломке, используемой бизнес-консультантами в 70-х и 80-х годах. Необходимо было соединить 9 точек, используя при этом лишь 4 прямые непрерывные линии и не отрывая карандаш от листа бумаги. Единственное верное решение – провести линии за пределами квадрата. Таким образом, чтобы справиться со сложной задачей, вы должны уметь «мыслить за пределами ограничительных рамок».

for the record – *see Lesson 4*

(to) share the credit – to acknowledge someone else's contribution; to share with somebody else recognition for a job well done
отметить чей-то вклад; разделить с кем-либо признание, одобрение за хорошо проделанную работу

➤ Thank you for giving me the award for coming up with the best new product idea this year. But I really need to **share the credit** with my colleagues in the marketing department.

to give one a run for one's money – to be strong competition; to take business away from
составить кому-то серьезную конкуренцию; перебить чей-то бизнес

➤ When Yahoo decided to go into the online search business, they gave Google a **run for their money**.

Происхождение. Это выражение пришло из терминологии скачек. Так говорят о лошади, на которую были сделаны ставки и которая хорошо прошла дистанцию, однако не заняла призового места.

☜ PRACTICE THE IDIOMS

Выберите наиболее подходящий ответ к каждому предложению:

1) Our store had a very successful holiday season this year. Sales were through the roof!
   a) I'm sorry to hear that you need a new roof.
   b) That's great. Congratulations!
   c) Don't worry. Maybe next year will be better.

2) We're looking for some fresh thinking in our marketing department. Are you good at thinking outside the box?
   a) Yes, I tend to think like everybody else.
   b) Yes, I enjoy approaching new projects in a traditional way.
   c) Yes, I'm great at coming up with new and creative ideas.

3) I'd like to share the credit with you. Without you, I wouldn't have been able to find this important new client.
   a) Thank you. I appreciate the recognition.
   b) Thanks, but I already have enough credit.
   c) I think I deserve some of the credit too.

4) A big Ace Hardware store is opening up in town. Do you think they'll give our local hardware store a run for their money?
   a) Definitely. Their selection will be bigger and their prices may be lower.
   b) Yes, our local hardware store will definitely run out of money.
   c) No. Everybody in town will start shopping at Ace Hardware.

5) Since you need to drum up some new business, I suggest you exhibit at a trade show.
   a) We don't have any business right now.
   b) We've been thinking about going into the drum business.
   c) Great idea! I'm sure we could find some new clients there.

6) You deserve a pat on the back for figuring out how to fix our computer network.
   a) Thanks. It was my pleasure.
   b) Thanks. Let me turn around so you can see my back.
   c) Sorry. I wish I could've done a better job.

7) Kudos to you and the rest of the manufacturing department for figuring out how to cut our production costs!
   a) We don't need any more kudos. We have enough in inventory.
   b) Thank you. We are proud of our results.
   c) We'll try our best, but we can't guarantee anything.

8) Traditional ways of advertising are no longer working for our firm. Do you think we should try some guerrilla marketing?
   a) Absolutely. It's always better to use reliable old methods.
   b) Yes, new ways of marketing might help increase sales.
   c) No, I think you should try marketing to monkeys instead.

ANSWERS TO LESSON 6, p. 191

We're in deep trouble. Sales are down by 50 percent.

DISCUSSING BAD RESULTS

Ron, Alex, and Pam work for Brooklyn Brewski, a company that brews and distributes beer throughout New York. The company's recent results have been terrible.

Рон, Алекс и Пэм работают в компании Brooklyn Brewski, которая специализируется на производстве и продаже пива в Нью-Йорке. В последнее время результаты коммерческой деятельности фирмы были явно неутешительными.

Alex: We need to **face the music** here. We're **in deep trouble**! Sales are down by 50 percent versus last year.

Pam: It looks like we're going to be **in the red** for the year **to the tune of** $1 million.

Ron: **No wonder**. We're losing **market share** to Manhattan Beer.

Alex: Why? We need to **get to the bottom of** this!

Pam: Every year they come up with new beers. They're really **on top of trends**. For instance, last year they released a *low-carb* beer.

Ron: **No wonder** they're **eating our lunch**! They're **cashing in on** the latest trends and **bringing great new products to market**.

Pam: Meanwhile, we're **running in place**. We need a new *product line* and new ideas for marketing.

Alex: It's time to **clean house** and bring some **new blood** into this company.

Ron: **You took the words right out of my mouth!** We need some new people with fresh ideas.

IDIOMS & EXPRESSIONS – LESSON 7

(to) face the music – to admit that there's a problem; to deal with an unpleasant situation realistically
признать наличие проблемы; реалистично оценивать кризисную ситуацию; встречать, не дрогнув, критику или трудности

➤ Enron executives finally had to **face the music** and admit that they were involved in some illegal activities.

in deep trouble – having a serious problem; in crisis
сталкиваться с серьезными неприятностями; быть в тяжелой или кризисной ситуации

➤ If there's another winter without any snowfall, Craig's snow plowing business is going to be **in deep trouble**.

in the red – *see Lesson 2*

to the tune of (followed by a number) – in the amount of; approximately
в размере; на сумму; приблизительно (далее следуют цифры)

➤ This year, our Beijing office will bring in revenues **to the tune of** two million dollars.

no wonder – it's not surprising that
неудивительно, что; немудрено, что

➤ **No wonder** Randy hasn't been promoted in 10 years. He just sits in his office surfing the Internet all day.

market share   the percentage of sales a company has in relation to its competitors for a product or product line
доля рынка, т.е. соотношение между объемом продаж одной компании и объемом продаж всех других компаний в конкретном сегменте рынка; процент продаж компании по определенному виду товара или линии продукции в сравнении с конкурентами

➤ We're in trouble. Our **market share** went from 50 percent last year to only 20 percent this year!

Примечание. См. ниже глаголы, которые наиболее часто сочетаются со словами **market share**:

(to) gain market share – to increase one's share of the market.
расширить свою долю рынка; увеличить занимаемую долю рынка

➤ With the launch of their popular new herbal toothpaste, Colgate **gained market share**. (Фирма Colgate значительно расширила свою долю рынка, запустив в продажу новую популярную зубную пасту с травяными добавками).

(to) lose market share – to decrease one's share of the market
утратить, потерять, уступить, понизить свою долю рынка

➤ Last year, Internet Explorer **lost market share** to one of its rivals, Mozilla. (В прошедшем году Internet Explorer уступил свою долю рынка одному из своих конкурентов – Mozilla).

(to) steal market share (from) – to take sales away from a competitor
завоевать, захватить, овладеть долей рынка конкурента

➤ Motorola and Samsung are trying to **steal market share from** Nokia. (Motorola и Samsung пытаются овладеть долей рынка Nokia).

(to) get to the bottom of something – to figure out what's going on; to find out what's causing a problem
докопаться до сути; разобраться, в чем проблема

➤ When hundreds of people had heart attacks after taking Zylestra's new prescription drug, the Federal Drug Administration promised to **get to the bottom of it**.

on top of trends – modern; aware and responding to the latest tastes
современный; отвечающий новейшим требованиям

➤ The Gap is **on top of trends**. They always have the latest styles in their stores.

eating one's lunch – taking away one's business
«съесть чужой ленч»: перехватить у кого-то бизнес; обскакать кого-либо

➤ Ever since Wal-Mart came into town, our local stores have been doing poorly. Wal-Mart is **eating their lunch**.

(to) cash in on – to make money on; to benefit financially from
заработать на чем-либо; извлечь выгоду из чего-либо; обращать в свою пользу

➤ Jamie Oliver, star of the TV show *The Naked Chef,* **cashed in on** his popularity by writing cookbooks and opening restaurants.

(to) bring a product to market – to introduce or launch a new product
представить или запустить на рынок новый продукт

➤ Next year will be very busy for Procter & Gamble's Oil of Olay division. They're going to **bring many new products to market**.

(to) run in place – to not make any progress; to be stuck; to remain in the same place for a long period of time
топтаться на месте; застопориться (о каком-либо деле); не добиться успеха

➤ Our company needs to come up with some innovative new products. We've been **running in place** for years.

(to) clean house – to fire a lot of employees
уволить большое кол-во служащих; «провести чистку»

➤ The airline was nearly bankrupt. They had no choice but to **clean house**.

new blood – new employees
«молодая кровь»; новое пополнение; новые сотрудники

➤ When the biotech company brought some **new blood** into their R&D department, their business really started to improve.

You took the words right out of my mouth!
I completely agree with you; I was just going to say that
я полностью с вами согласен; именно это я и собирался сказать; вы читаете мои мысли; у меня это вертелось на языке

➤ "I hope the boss doesn't hold our holiday party at his house again this year." — "**You took the words right out of my mouth!** I'd much rather go to a restaurant."

⚑ PRACTICE THE IDIOMS

Заполните пропуски, используя следующие идиомы:

new blood
in deep trouble
no wonder
running in place
eating their lunch
face the music
on top of trends
bring some new products to market

Zylestra is a large pharmaceutical company. They haven't introduced any major new drugs in a long time. They've been _____(1)_____ for the past few years. Their biggest competitor, Delmar Drugs, is stealing market share from them and is _____(2)_____. It's _____(3)_____ Delmar is more successful. In the past few years, they've come out with effective drugs for lowering cholesterol and reducing the risk of heart disease. Delmar understands what their customers want. They invest heavily in consumer research to stay _____(4)_____. Meanwhile, Zylestra is still selling the same drugs it was selling three years ago. If Zylestra doesn't follow Delmar's example and _____(5)_____ soon, they're going to be _____(6)_____. Investors in the company hope that Richard Pierce, Zylestra's CEO, will _____(7)_____ and take action to turn around the company. As a first step, he should bring in some _____(8)_____ to help him run the company.

ANSWERS TO LESSON 7, p. 191

I recommend we bite the bullet and move our operations to China.

DISCUSSING A DIFFICULT DECISION

Anna, Lynn, and Jeff are thinking about moving their manufacturing facilities from the United States to China. Jeff is having trouble deciding what to do.

Анна, Линн и Джеф подумывают о переводе производственных предприятий из США в Китай. Джефу трудно принять окончательное решение.

Anna: We need to decide already whether or not we want to move our manufacturing from the United States to China. Jeff, have you made the final decision?

Jeff: There are *pros and cons* to moving it to China. I've been **back and forth on this issue** for months. I'm **of two minds**.

Anna: Jeff, I know this is a **tough call**, but now is not the time to be **wishy-washy**. We need to make a decision.

Lynn: That's right, and I recommend we **bite the bullet** and move our operations to China.

Anna: Or we could **test the waters** by moving 25 percent of our operations there.

Lynn: Good idea. That would give us **the best of both worlds**: we could reduce our risk, while starting to enjoy some of the cost savings from lower-cost manufacturing.

Jeff: I agree with you that we should **put a stake in the ground**. Let's move a quarter of our operations to China.

Lynn: **Good call**, Jeff!

IDIOMS & EXPRESSIONS – LESSON 8

back and forth on an issue – repeatedly changing one's mind about something; having trouble settling on an opinion or decision
постоянно менять точку зрения; колебаться с приятием решения; не иметь определенного мнения о чем-либо

> Should we change our company health care plan? I can't make up my mind. I go **back and forth on the issue**.

of two minds – conflicted about something
нет единого мнения; конфликтные, противоречивые представления о чем-либо

> Many consumers are **of two minds** about buying organic produce. On the one hand, it is often more expensive than regular produce. On the other hand, it may be healthier.

tough call – a difficult decision; something difficult to predict
трудное решение; то, что трудно предвидеть или предсказать

> It was a **tough call**, but the company finally decided to close down its operations in Mexico.

wishy-washy – ineffective; lacking will-power; indecisive; incapable of making clear decisions
неэффективный; безвольный; нерешительный; неспособный принимать четкие решения; ни то ни се; ни рыба ни мясо

> Wendy is **wishy-washy**. She changed her mind a hundred times about which packaging design to use for the new product.

(to) bite the bullet – to make a difficult or painful decision; to take a difficult step
принимать трудное или мучительное решение; решиться на трудный шаг

> When demand was down, U.S. automakers had to **bite the bullet** and cut jobs.

Происхождение. Эта идиома пришла из военного лексикона. В период Гражданкой войны в США врачи во время операции часто использовали виски для анестезии. Если виски кончались, раненому солдату клали пулю в рот, и он буквально «кусал пулю зубами». Судя по всему, это действовало как отвлекающее средство, помогая притупить боль и облегчить тем самым физические страдания.

(to) test the waters – to try something out before committing to it; to see what the response or outcome will be to an intended action
разведать обстановку; прощупать почву; посмотреть, каков будет результат, прежде чем принять окончательное решение

➤ Before quitting his job as a lawyer to become a chef, Chad **tested the waters** by working weekends at a restaurant.

the best of both worlds – a situation or product that offers two very different advantages at the same time
ситуация или товар, которые имеют двойное преимущество, представляют двойную выгоду

➤ BMW's new sports car offers **the best of both worlds**: a reliable car that's also fun to drive.

(to) put a stake in the ground – to take the first step; to make a big move to get something started; to make a commitment
сделать первый шаг; предпринять что-либо для запуска проекта; взять на себя обязательства, ответственность

➤ Our business in California has grown steadily over the past two years. Now is the time to **put a stake in the ground** and open a regional office there.

good call – good decision
правильное решение; верный шаг

➤ **Good call** on buying Google stock. It has gone way up since you bought it.

(to) live to regret a decision – to feel bad later about one's decision
сожалеть впоследствии о принятом ранее решении; кусать себе локти

➤ The mayor agreed to allow a new dump to be built in town, but he later **lived to regret his decision**.

my gut tells me – I have a strong feeling that; my intuition tells me
нутром чувствовать; моя интуиция подсказывает мне

➤ It's true that I don't know him well, but **my gut tells me** that Max is the right person for the sales director position.

Примечание. Слово "gut" означает «внутренности, кишки».

✎ Practice the Idioms

Найдите наилучшую замену выделенным выражениям:

1) Sandra **is of two minds about** leaving her job to get an MBA.
   a) is upset about
   b) isn't sure about
   c) is very positive about

2) You decided to invest some money in real estate? **Good call!**
   a) You're a good person!
   b) I'll call you back!
   c) Good idea!

3) Ford Motor Company debated for a long time whether or not to start making cars in Russia, but the company finally decided to **bite the bullet**.
   a) drop the project
   b) go ahead with it
   c) enter the weapons business

4) I know you're nervous about the launch of our new robotic vacuum cleaner, but **my gut tells me** it's going to be a big seller.
   a) I have a strong feeling that
   b) my friend tells me that
   c) I don't think that

5) Janet left her old job before finding a new one and **lived to regret her decision**.
   a) had trouble finding a new job
   b) was happy with her decision
   c) was sorry about it later

6) Unfortunately, our company president is not a great leader. He's **wishy-washy**.
   a) inconsiderate
   b) not good at making decisions
   c) lazy

7) Kate says running a business from her home **gives her the best of both worlds**: she can stay at home with her four young children and still make some money.
   a) allows her all possible advantages
   b) gives her more work than she can handle
   c) lets her stay at home all day doing nothing

8) The computer store was unsure at first how much demand there would be for the new line of laptops, so they started with a small order to **test the waters**.
   a) make sure the laptops really worked
   b) see if there was demand for the laptops
   c) see if customers were interested in buying water

ANSWERS TO LESSON 8, p. 191

This website is a far cry from what we were expecting.

DEALING WITH A DISSATISFIED CUSTOMER

John hired Kevin's web design firm to design a website for his company, but John is not satisfied with the end result.

Джон воспользовался услугами дизайнерской фирмы Kevin's web design для разработки сайта своей компании, но остался недоволен конечным результатом.

John: We're disappointed with the website you designed for us. It's **a far cry from** what we were expecting.

Kevin: I'm sorry you're not satisfied. We really **went all out** to make it a great site.

John: Well, I'm not going to **mince words**, but you charged us a **pretty penny** and you didn't **deliver**.

Kevin: Wow, I'm really surprised to hear you say that! We **pulled out all the stops**.

John: Don't try to **pull the wool over my eyes**. You promised that your best people would work on this project, but our website looks like it was designed by a *summer intern!*

Kevin: What exactly is the problem with the site?

John: **Where to begin?** The *shopping cart* doesn't even work.

Kevin: Really? Well, we'll **get right on that.**

John: And you guys **messed around** forever getting the site done. You were three months behind schedule!

Kevin: I'm sorry about that. We were **swamped**. Let me **make it up to you**. We'll give you a 25 percent discount on the project.

IDIOMS & EXPRESSIONS – LESSON 9

a far cry from – different than; not at all like; much less than
существенная разница; совершенно не похоже; быть далеким от
оригинала; небо и земля

> Cisco Systems' stock may be trading higher, but it's still **a far cry from** where it was in 2000.

(to) go all out – to make a big effort; to try hard
прилагать невероятные усилия; лезть из кожи вон; лечь костьми;
выбиваться из сил ради чего-то

> The small gift shop **went all out** on advertising in December, trying to increase its holiday sales.

(to) mince words – to control one's language so as to be polite
смягчать выражения; следить за своей речью, чтобы соблюсти
приличия

> Sue told you your new product idea was "the stupidest idea she's ever heard?" Clearly she's not one to **mince words**!

pretty penny – a lot of money; too much money (when referring to the cost of something)
изрядная или кругленькая сумма; хороший куш; слишком дорого
(если говорят о цене)

> Lisa made a **pretty penny** selling antiques on eBay.

(to) deliver – to meet the requirements of a task, project, or job
выполнить обязательства; сделать то, что ожидалось

> You made a lot of promises during your job interview here. Now that you're hired, I hope you can **deliver**!

(to) pull out all the stops – to use all one's resources to get something done; to try very hard
нажать на все кнопки; использовать все рычаги; сделать все
возможное для достижения цели; очень стараться

> Many airline companies are **pulling out all the stops** to win the right to fly direct to China.

Происхождение: Это выражение пришло из мира музыки. Одно
из значений "stop" – регистр органа. При помощи регистров
органисты добиваются полноты звучания органа.

(to) pull the wool over one's eyes – to deceive someone
обманывать; темнить; ввести кого-либо в заблуждение

➤ Are you telling me the truth, or are you trying to **pull the wool over my eyes**?

Происхождение. Это выражение восходит к 18-19 вв., к эпохе, когда мужчины носили парики. Слово "wool" в данном случае означает «парик из шерсти». Надвинутый на глаза, он лишал своего обладателя возможности видеть что-либо.

Where to begin? – There is so much to say, I have to think about where to start (usually used when you're about to complain and you want to stress that there's a lot to complain about).
С чего же начать? Столько надо высказать! Надо подумать, с чего начать. (Обычно употребляется, когда вы хотите подчеркнуть, что вам есть на что пожаловаться).

➤ Your new ad campaign has so many problems. **Where to begin?**

(to) get right on something – to take care of something immediately
принять немедленные меры; позаботиться о чем-либо без промедления

➤ You need my help in finding a new office to lease? I'll **get right on that**.

(to) mess around – to waste time; to spend time with no particular purpose or goal
лодырничать; слоняться без дела; убивать время; валять дурака

➤ We don't have time to **mess around** with the design for the packaging. Let's just design it quickly and get it into production!

(to be) swamped – to have too much work to do; to be very busy
быть заваленным работой; быть очень занятым

➤ Accounting firms are **swamped** during tax season.

(to) make it up to you – to do something to compensate you for your trouble
сделать что-либо, чтобы возместить чьи-то затраты, потери или неудобства; сделать все, что вы пожелаете

➤ I'm sorry you weren't happy with the sign we made for you. Let me **make it up to you** and make you a new sign at no charge.

☜ PRACTICE THE IDIOMS

Заполните пропуски, используя следующие идиомы:

mince words	**pretty penny**
pull the wool over my eyes	**deliver**
make it up to you	**Where to begin**
a far cry from	**pulled out all the stops**

Linda: We're never going to use Donna's Delights Catering again! You promised you'd do a great job with our holiday party, but you didn't _____(1)_____ .

Donna: Oh, really? What exactly was the problem?

Linda: _____(2)_____ ? There were so many problems! First of all, the main course was _____(3)_____ what we were expecting. I'm not going to _____(4)_____ . The steak you served us tasted like rubber!

Donna: I'm really surprised. I put my best chef on this project, and we bought the best steak available. We _____(5)_____ .

Linda: I have a feeling you're trying to _____(6)_____ . I know my steak, and I know the steak you served was low quality.

Donna: Well, I guess it's possible we ordered the wrong meat.

Linda: You charged us a _____(7)_____ for your services, and you did a lousy job. We won't be using your company anymore.

Donna: I'm sorry. Let me _____(8)_____ . We'll bring free lunch for your entire office next Friday.

ANSWERS TO LESSON 9, p. 191

DISCUSSING A DIFFICULT REQUEST

Tanya is a head of R&D in a laboratory for Sudsco, a company that makes shampoo. Here she meets with colleagues John and Andy to discuss a request from the marketing department.

Таня возглавляет отдел исследований и разработок в лаборатории фирмы Sudsco, выпускающей шампуни. Она встречается в Джоном и Энди, чтобы обсудить запрос, полученный из отдела по маркетингу.

Tanya: Let me **kick off** this meeting with some news. Our marketing department would like us to produce a new fragrance by the end of next month.

John: Oh, brother.* We **need this extra work like a hole in the head!** What fragrance are they looking for?

Tanya: Mango.

Andy: Mango? Are they out of their minds? Do they know how *tough* that is?

Tanya: Yeah, but I told them we'd **take a crack at it**. If we **put our minds to it**, I know we can do it.

Andy: I don't know. It's not going to be easy.

Tanya: Let's **roll up our sleeves** and **give it our best shot**. **Nothing ventured, nothing gained**.

John: Well, Tanya, you certainly have a **can-do attitude**!

Tanya: Actually, this is **child's play** compared to what our CEO wants us to do by the end of the year. He wants us to come up with new, improved formulas for all 50 of our shampoos.

Andy: What? How are we supposed to manage that? Sometimes I think the **bigwigs** at this company are **out of touch with reality**!

* oh, brother – восклицание, выражающее досаду или изумление

IDIOMS & EXPRESSIONS – LESSON 10

(to) kick off – to start something, such as a meeting or a project
начинать что-либо (встречу, проект); браться за какое-либо дело или проект

➤ Bill Gates **kicked off** the conference by showing a demonstration of Microsoft's new search engine.

Примечание. Вы можете также встретить фразу "kick-off meeting" – стартовое собрание или совещание, знаменующее начало работы над новым проектом.

(to) need something like a hole in the head – to have no need for something; to have no desire for something
не испытывать нужды в чем-либо; не иметь желания делать что-либо; нужно, как в голове дырка, как прошлогодний снег, как рыбе зонтик

➤ One of our competitors is threatening to take us to court. We **need that like a hole in the head**!

---

out of one's mind – crazy; having unrealistic thoughts or ideas
быть не в своем уме; лишиться рассудка; тешить себя несбыточными идеями или мечтами

➤ Our DSL provider is telling us that our rates will go up by 50 percent starting next month. Are they **out of their minds**?

(to) take a crack at something – to try something
делать попытки; пробовать на зуб

➤ It's going to be hard for us to lower our raw materials cost on this product, but we'll **take a crack at it**.

Synonym: to have a go at something

(to) put one's mind to something – to focus on a task; to try hard to do something

вбить что-либо в голову; сфокусироваться на задаче; полностью сконцентрироваться на каком-либо деле

> Your accounting course may be difficult, but if you **put your mind to it**, you'll get through it.

(to) roll up one's sleeves – to get ready to start something; to prepare to do something

взяться за работу засучив рукава; подготовиться к какому-либо делу

> We've got to pack up 500 crystal vases by tomorrow morning, so let's **roll up our sleeves** and get to work.

(to) give it one's best shot – to make one's best effort to get something done; to try to do something, even though you're not sure if you'll be successful

приложить максимальное усилие; сделать лучшее, на что способен, даже если нет уверенности в успехе предприятия

> The small brewery went out of business after three unprofitable years, but at least they **gave it their best shot**.

---

nothing ventured, nothing gained – If you don't try to do something, you'll never succeed.

кто не рискует, тот не выигрывает; риск – благородное дело; кто не рискует, тот не пьет шампанского; волков бояться – в лес не ходить

> It's risky to spend so much money developing a new brand, but **nothing ventured, nothing gained**.

Примечание. Глагол "to venture" означает «идти на риск», «ставить на карту», решиться на что-либо, отважиться.

---

can-do attitude – a positive way of looking at things; an optimistic perspective; a positive attitude

позитивный взгляд на вещи; уверенность в будущем; нет ничего невозможного

> Marie always says that nothing's impossible. She's got a real **can-do attitude**.

child's play – an easy task
детские игры; пустяковое дело; проще простого; пара пустяков

> Victor has been an auto mechanic for 20 years, so replacing your windshield wipers will be **child's play** for him.

---

bigwig – very important person; person in charge
важная персона; большая шишка; ответственное лицо

> All the **bigwigs** from the company went to Hawaii for a four-day conference.

SYNONYMS: head honcho; big cheese; VIP (very important person)

Происхождение. Это выражение произошло от "big wig" – «большой парик», что было атрибутом мужской моды в старой Англии. По размеру парика можно было судить о положении в обществе его владельца: важные персоны носили самые большие парики.

---

out of touch with reality – unrealistic; not aware of what's really going on
оторванный от реальности; витающий в облаках; не от мира сего

> The CEO believes his company's stock price will triple in a year. Most people think he's **out of touch with reality**.

✎ PRACTICE THE IDIOMS

Найдите наилучшую замену выделенным выражениям:

1) Our president gave everybody business card holders for Christmas. **I need another business card holder like a hole in the head.**
   a) I really need a new business card holder.
   b) I'm happy to get another business card holder.
   c) I really don't need another business card holder.

2) Installing that new computer software was **child's play** for Mark. He's got a PhD in computer science.
   a) very easy
   b) challenging
   c) enjoyable

3) I agree with you that we may not be successful entering the market in China, but **nothing ventured, nothing gained**.
   a) we should take a risk and enter the Chinese market
   b) we shouldn't enter the Chinese market
   c) if we enter the Chinese market, we'll definitely succeed

4) If you can't figure out how to fix the jammed printer, let Adam **take a crack at it**.
   a) fix the crack in it
   b) try to fix it
   c) throw it in the trash

5) The company **kicked off** the new fiscal year by announcing several exciting new products.
   a) ended
   b) postponed
   c) began

6) It won't be easy, but if you **put your mind to it**, you can study for your law degree while also working full-time.
   a) don't think too much about it
   b) work hard at it
   c) think about it

7) Sorry I couldn't get you the financial reports by Friday. I **gave it my best shot**, but I just couldn't finish on time.
   a) tried as hard as I could
   b) made a little effort
   c) didn't try too hard

8) If you want to work for IBM, call my cousin Alan. He's a **bigwig** there.
   a) low-level employee
   b) frequent visitor
   c) senior executive

ANSWERS TO LESSON 10, p. 191

REVIEW FOR LESSONS 6-10

Вставьте пропущенные слова:

1) We're not happy with our accounting firm. All of the mistakes they made with our taxes cost us a pretty _____.

   a) nickel   b) penny   c) dollar

2) If the pharmaceutical company's new product is not approved by the Food and Drug Administration, they're going to be _____ deep trouble.

   a) with   b) on   c) in

3) Sales will probably be slow after the holidays. Let's think of a way to _____ up some business.

   a) beat   b) break   c) drum

4) Olivia is _____ two minds about quitting her job and starting her own business. On the one hand, it will be more exciting. On the other hand, she's afraid of taking a risk.

   a) of   b) with   c) at

5) In the months following Google's initial public offering, the stock price went _____ the roof.

   a) up   b) out   c) through

6) Your business has grown too large to run out of your home. You're going to need to _____ the bullet and rent some office space.

   a) eat   b) bite   c) take

7) Our CEO kicked _____ the company holiday party by warning people not to drink too much champagne.

   a) off   b) out   c) in

8) If you want to bring some _____ blood into the company, put an advertisement on Monster.com or another online job search site.

    a) red   b) smart   c) new

9) Jerry doesn't understand what's going on in the marketplace today. He's _____ touch with reality.

    a) out of   b) close to   c) far from

10) Don't mince _____. Tell Heather what you *really* think about her performance.

    a) words   b) language   c) talk

11) Irene wasn't sure she'd be able to prepare the financial reports by tomorrow's meeting, but she promised to _____ a crack at it.

    a) make   b) take   c) do

12) Ben pulled out all the _____ to ensure that his business partner from Chile enjoyed his visit to the United States.

    a) starts   b) stops   c) tricks

13) We've got a lot of employees just sitting around and playing Solitaire on their computers all day. It's time to _____ house.

    a) wash   b) clean   c) empty

14) If we don't roll _____ our sleeves and get started on this project, we're going to miss our deadline.

    a) down   b) out   c) up

15) Apple is a very innovative company. They're always dreaming _____ interesting new products.

    a) about   b) up   c) down

ANSWERS TO REVIEW, p. 192

I'll count on you two to rally the troops.

MOTIVATING CO-WORKERS

Greg, Stan, and Donna work for Pack-It, a maker of trash bags and other consumer goods. After disappointing sales results, they discuss exiting the trash bag business. But a fresh new idea gives them hope for the future.

Грег, Стэн и Донна работают в компании Pack-It, выпускающей мешки для мусора и другие товары широкого потребления. Получив неутешительные результаты о ходе продаж, они обсуждают возможность выхода из бизнеса по производству мусорных мешков. Однако новая, свежая идея вселяет в них надежду на будущее.

Greg: Our sales were down again last quarter.

Donna: We've been **working our tails off** and our results are still lousy!

Greg: Maybe we should exit the trash bag business — just **call it quits**!

Stan: C'mon.* Let's not **throw in the towel** yet. **We've been down before, but we always come back fighting**.

Donna: But this time *private-label products* are **driving us out of business**!

Stan: We've got a successful **track record**. Everybody knows that we offer quality trash bags.

Donna: That's true, but we can't just **rest on our laurels** forever.

Stan: Well, I have a new idea that's going to **turn around our business**.

It's a new line of trash bags that smell like fresh fruits such as apples and peaches.

Greg: That sounds like a great idea. I'm ready to **roll up my sleeves and get down to business!**

Stan: I appreciate your **team spirit**! Donna, are you **on board** too?

Donna: Sure. **Count me in**.

Stan: Great. Let's get everybody else in the company excited about this plan too. I'll count on you two to **rally the troops**.

* C'mon – краткая разговорная форма от come on. Здесь в значении: «Подожди! Послушай!». Часто употребляется как побуждение к действию: «Ну, давай! Живей! Продолжай!».

IDIOMS & EXPRESSIONS – LESSON 11

(to) work one's tail off – to work very hard
работать не покладая рук; работать день и ночь; вкалывать

➤ The software developers **worked their tails off** to get the new software package released before Christmas.

(to) call it quits – to give up; to quit; to stop; to admit defeat
отказаться от чего-либо; бросить, прекратить делать что-либо; признать поражение

➤ When Borders announced they were building a new bookstore in town, the small book shop decided to **call it quits**.

(to) throw in the towel – to give up; to surrender; to admit defeat; капитулировать; сдаться; признать поражение

➤ After several years of trying to run a small business from his home, Peter finally decided to **throw in the towel**.

Происхождение. Это идиома пришла из боксерского лексикона. Когда боксер проигрывал бой, его ассистент выбрасывал полотенце на ринг в знак признания поражения и окончания поединка. Это было то самое полотенце, которым вытирали пот и кровь с лица боксера во время боя.

We've been down before, but we always come back fighting.
Everything is going to be okay; we've had trouble in the past too, and we managed to get over that
Все образуется; у нас и раньше были трудные времена, но мы смогли все преодолеть

> We need to be optimistic about our future. **We've been down before, but we always come back fighting.**

---

track record – a record of achievement or performances
история прошлых результатов; список прежних достижений и успехов; послужной список

> General Electric has a proven **track record** of making successful acquisitions.

(to) rest on one's laurels – to believe that past success is enough to guarantee that the future will also be successful; to rely too much on reputation
почивать на лаврах; полагать, что успех в прошлом может служить гарантией успеха в будущем

> The CEO made several positive changes during his first five years with the company, but now many people say he's just **resting on his laurels**.

Происхождение. Во времена Древнего Рима лавровый венец считался символом победы и успеха.

(to) turn around one's business – to make a business profitable again; to go from not making profits to being profitable again
поднять прибыльность бизнеса; вывести бизнес из категории убыточного, превратив его снова в прибыльный

> The telecom company was able to **turn around its business** by developing a popular new line of services.

(to) roll up one's sleeves – *see Lesson 10*

(to) get down to business – to start work; to begin discussing the important issues
уделить внимание бизнесу; браться за дело; переходить ближе к делу; вернуться к обсуждению деловых вопросов

➤ We could talk about last night's baseball game for hours, but let's **get down to business** and start the negotiation.

---

team spirit – enthusiasm; enthusiasm about doing something for the group
энтузиазм; умение работать в коллективе; чувство локтя

➤ Jill is always organizing company trips and lunches. She's got a lot of **team spirit**.

---

on board – ready to participate; in agreement (with a plan or a suggestion)
быть готовым к участию; согласиться с условиями

➤ Before we agree to sign this contract with our new partner, we'd better make sure our president is **on board**.

---

count me in – I will participate.
Я – за. Можете на меня рассчитывать.

➤ You're organizing a goodbye party for Christine? **Count me in**.

(to) rally the troops – to motivate others; to get other people excited about doing something; to do something to improve the morale of the employees and get them energized about doing their work
побуждать, стимулировать других; поднять моральный дух в коллективе; передать свой энтузиазм другим

➤ After the lay-offs and salary cuts, the airline president held a meeting to **rally the troops** and plan for the next year.

Примечание. Глагол "to rally" имеет несколько значений. В данном случае – «призывать к общему делу, объединяться, сплачиваться». "Troops" – неформальное название рабочего коллектива. Этот термин пришел из военного лексикона и означает «воинская часть, подразделение».

✍ PRACTICE THE IDIOMS

Заполните пропуски, используя следующие идиомы:

track record	**on board**
count me in	**team spirit**
rally the troops	**turn around our business**
throw in the towel	**working their tails off**

Kim: Sales at our Westport furniture store are down by 50 percent this year. I've got a plan to ____(1)____ . For the month of December, we'll stand on street corners with big signs advertising our store.

Jason: Stand on street corners in this cold weather? Maybe we should just ____(2)____ and close the Westport store. Our other five stores are still doing well.

Cindy: Kim, I like your idea. I'm ready to participate. ____(3)____ !

Mark: I'm ____(4)____ too.

Cindy: I'd be happy to ____(5)____ and get all of our other employees to join us, starting with Jason.

Kim: Yeah, Jason. Where's your ____(6)____ ? Everybody else is going to participate.

Mark: Right, Jason. You're going to feel guilty when everybody else is ____(7)____ outside while you're inside drinking coffee and relaxing.

Jason: Okay, I'll do it. I just can't believe that with our excellent ____(8)____ , we now have to take such desperate action!

ANSWERS TO LESSON 11, p. 192

Let's get down to business.

RUNNING A MEETING

Julia is running a meeting. When Larry and Sally start arguing, Julia has to bring the meeting back under control.

Юлия ведет совещание. Когда Ларри и Салли начинают спорить, Юлия старается вернуть проведение собрания под свой контроль.

Julia: Let's **get down to business**. We need to **cover a lot of ground**. Our first *agenda item* is to figure out how we're going to respond to all the complaints we've been getting about our new website.

Larry: Just so we're all **on the same page**, please give us an *overview* of the problem.

Julia: **In a nutshell**, our customers are complaining that it's very difficult to place orders through the new website.

Sally: I think we **jumped the gun** by not conducting *focus groups* with our customers before we *launched our new website*.

Larry: More focus groups? **Every time I turn around** we're running focus groups! It's **gotten out of hand**.

Sally: **I beg to differ**. Focus groups are very important. They help us better understand our customer.

Julia: Well, clearly you two **don't see eye-to-eye** on this issue.

Larry: Ha! **That's putting it lightly**! Focus groups are a waste of time and...

Julia: Excuse me, let's not **get off track** here. Does anybody else want to **weigh in on the issue at hand**?

Carl: If I can **put in my two cents**, I agree with Sally that focus groups would've been a good idea.

Julia: Well, enough about focus groups for now. Let's **move on** to our next *agenda item* — planning for our *company offsite*.

Larry: Wait, I'm not finished talking about the website!

Julia: We can **circle back to** that at the end of our meeting if we have time. I want to keep us on schedule since I know many of us have another meeting at 11 o'clock.

IDIOMS & EXPRESSIONS – LESSON 12

(to) get down to business – *see Lesson 11*

(to) cover a lot of ground – to discuss many topics; to have a productive discussion
затронуть множество тем; провести плодотворную дискуссию

➤ That was an excellent meeting. We **covered a lot of ground**.

(to be) on the same page – *see Lesson 5*

---

in a nutshell – in summary; in short
вкратце; подводя итог; короче говоря

➤ I won't go into the details now. **In a nutshell**, our sales are down 50 percent versus one year ago.

(to) jump the gun – to start doing something too soon or ahead of everybody else
совершить фальстарт (в легкой атлетике); начать действовать преждевременно или раньше других

➤ The company **jumped the gun** by releasing a new product before the results of the consumer testing were in.

Происхождение. Это выражение из спортивной лексики: когда бегун начинает движение до выстрела стартового пистолета.

every time I turn around – frequently; too often
зачастую; слишком часто; когда ни взглянешь

➤ **Every time I turn around**, Lisa is checking her stock portfolio on Yahoo. No wonder she never gets any work done.

(to be or to get) out of hand – to be too much; to be out of control
выходить из под контроля; отбиваться от рук; становиться неуправляемым

➤ Jake has called in sick 10 times this month. The situation is **getting out of hand**.

I beg to differ – I don't agree
Позвольте с вами не согласиться (официальная форма выражения несогласия).

➤ You think Tim has the leadership skills required to run this division? **I beg to differ!**

(to) not see eye-to-eye – to not be in agreement
расходиться во мнениях; не быть в согласии

➤ Our manufacturing and our marketing people fight with each other all the time. They **don't see eye-to-eye** on anything.

that's putting it lightly – that's definitely true; that's for sure; that's an understatement
это сущая правда; точно, наверняка; без всяких недомолвок

➤ "You were upset when your husband lost his job?" — **"That's putting it lightly!"**

(to) get off track – to get off the subject; to lose focus; to digress
потерять фокус; потерять нить; отвлекаться, отклоняться от темы

➤ We've **gotten off track**. This meeting was supposed to be about our new sales strategy, but we ended up talking about Erin's vacation in Spain!

(to) weigh in on – to say something about; to comment on; to express an opinion
высказаться по какому-либо поводу; выразить мнение или прокомментировать что-либо

➤ We'd like you to **weigh in on** some ideas we have for new products.

the issue at hand – the topic under discussion; what's being talked about now

тема обсуждения; то, что сейчас в центре внимания; животрепещущая тема

➤ We've somehow gotten off the topic. Let's return to **the issue at hand**.

(to) put in one's two cents – to offer one's opinion; to give an opinion without being asked

предложить свое мнение; высказать мнение без надобности

➤ Let me just **put in my two cents** and say that I think we should definitely move our manufacturing to China.

(to) move on
1) to proceed
двигаться дальше; переходить к чему-либо новому

➤ It's time we **move on** to our next topic.

2) to leave a job and do something else
оставить работу и заняться каким-либо другим делом

➤ Don't feel too bad that you were fired. It was probably time for you to **move on** anyway.

(to) circle back to – to return to
вернуться к чему-либо; вернуться на круги своя

➤ I'd like to **circle back** to something Ed said earlier in the meeting.

✎ PRACTICE THE IDIOMS

Найдите наилучшую замену выделенным выражениям:

1) Jim thinks his company should outsource its customer service to India, but his boss thinks they should keep it in California. **They don't see eye-to-eye on the issue.**
   a) They don't understand the issue.
   b) They don't agree on the issue.
   c) They agree on the issue.

2) We're going to conduct focus groups so consumers can **weigh in on** the design of some of our new products.
   a) complain about
   b) dictate
   c) give their opinion on

3) I know we're in a hurry to end the meeting, but let me just **circle back to** something David said earlier.
   a) emphasize
   b) return to
   c) dismiss

4) **Every time I turn around**, Ellen and Kelly are chatting.
   a) very frequently
   b) whenever I turn my back
   c) from time to time

5) **Let's not jump the gun** by buying a new printer before we can see if the old one can be fixed.
   a) let's not act too quickly
   b) let's take action now
   c) let's be efficient

6) I know many of you have more to say on this issue, but I'm afraid we're going to have to **move on** so we can finish this meeting on time.
   a) continue to discuss this
   b) leave the conference room now
   c) proceed to our next topic

7) Our office expenses are **out of hand**. We're going to have to stop spending so much.
   a) hard to count
   b) written down
   c) much too high

8) Calvin **covered a lot of ground** with his local partners during his business trip to Tokyo.
   a) saw much of the city
   b) had successful conversations
   c) made a lot of money

ANSWERS TO LESSON 12, p. 192

When filling out order forms, you need to dot your i's and cross your t's.

DISCUSSING A MISTAKE

Chris and Todd work for Alpine Design, a furniture manufacturer. When Todd accidentally orders the wrong amount of wood, his boss Chris warns him to be more careful in the future.

Крис и Тод работают в фирме Alpine Design, выпускающей мебель. Когда Тод по ошибке сделал неправильный заказ на лесоматериалы, его начальник Крис предупредил его о том, что надо быть более внимательным в будущем.

Chris: Todd, we got our shipment of wood yesterday. We're *short by* 18 tons.

Todd: Our wood supplier must've made a mistake. **I could've sworn that** I ordered the right amount.

Chris: You'd better go back and *double-check* your order.

Todd: Oops, you're right. I accidentally ordered two tons instead of twenty. **No big deal**. I'll just put in another order.

Chris: When filling out order forms, you need to **dot your i's and cross your t's**. You shouldn't be making careless mistakes like this.

Todd: I just forgot to add a zero after the two. Don't **make a mountain out of a molehill**. No need to **blow things out of proportion**.

Chris: This is very serious. Now we won't have enough wood to finish the furniture order we got from La-Z Boy.

Todd: Okay, sorry I **dropped the ball**.

Chris: Todd, this may be a **bitter pill to swallow**, but your work lately hasn't been **up to scratch**. You've really been **asleep at the wheel**!

IDIOMS & EXPRESSIONS – LESSON 13

I could've sworn that – I really thought that; I was convinced that
я мог бы поклясться, что; я действительно думал, что; я был уверен, что

➤ You didn't know we already hired somebody for the sales director position? **I could've sworn that** I told you.

Примечание. "Sworn" – это форма прошедшего времени от глагола "to swear" – «присягать, давать клятву».

no big deal – it's not a problem
это не проблема; не бог весть что; пустяки!

➤ Our coffee machine broke? **No big deal**. Our employees will just have to go to Starbucks until we get a new one.

(to) dot your i's and cross your t's – to be very careful; to pay close attention to details
ставить точки над i ; быть очень аккуратным; обращать пристальное внимание на детали

➤ When preparing financial statements, accuracy is very important. Be sure to **dot your i's and cross your t's**.

(to) make a mountain out of a molehill – to make a big deal out of something small or insignificant
сильно преувеличивать; делать из мухи слона; делать из блохи верблюда; сгущать краски

➤ Don't be angry at your boss for not complimenting you on your presentation. He probably just forgot. Don't **make a mountain out of a molehill**.

(to) blow things out of proportion – to exaggerate; to make more of something than one should
раздувать дело сверх меры; делать много шума из ничего

➤ Our CEO says that if we don't meet our sales target for the month, our company is going to go out of business. He's probably **blowing things out of proportion**.

(to) drop the ball – to make a mistake; to fail; to do something poorly

допустить промах, ошибку; попасть впросак; выпустить из рук инициативу; досл.: уронить мяч

➤ You forgot to submit the budget? You really **dropped the ball**!

Происхождение. Пришло из спортивной лексики: когда футболист упускает мяч, он лишается возможности изменить счет, так как мяч переходит к команде соперника.

---

bitter pill to swallow – bad news; something unpleasant to accept

горькая пилюля; плохие, неприятные новости

➤ After Gina spent her whole summer working as an intern for American Express, failing to get a full-time job offer from the company was a **bitter pill to swallow**.

---

up to scratch – good; at the expected level

на должной высоте; на ожидаемом уровне

➤ Your customer service call center isn't **up to scratch**. They put me on hold for 45 minutes!

Примечание. Обычно употребляется в негативной форме – not up to scratch

Происхождение. До того, как в боксе был официально принят гонг в качества сигнала к началу раунда, рефери чертил линию на ринге. Когда боксеры переступали эту линию, начинался раунд. Бой продолжался до тех пор, пока один из боксеров был не в состоянии подойти к черте: "not up to scratch".

SYNONYMS: up to par; up to speed

---

asleep at the wheel – not performing well; neglecting responsibilities; not paying attention to what's going on

спать на ходу; пренебрегать своими обязанностями; не следить за происходящим

➤ The dental hygienist was **asleep at the wheel**. She accidentally left a big piece of dental floss in the patient's mouth!

SYNONYMS: asleep at the switch; out to lunch

✎ PRACTICE THE IDIOMS

Заполните пропуски, используя следующие идиомы:

up to scratch	dot your i's and cross your t's
asleep at the wheel	I could've sworn that
bitter pill to swallow	no big deal
drop the ball	blow things out of proportion

Ryan: Eric, we got fifty phone calls this week complaining that our spicy nacho chips are much too spicy. Do you have the machine set correctly?

Eric: Let me check...No, we've got the machine set wrong. It's putting in three times too much hot pepper. That's strange. _____(1)_____ I checked it this morning and it was okay.

Ryan: Oh, for heaven's sake! How could you _____(2)_____ like this? You must be _____(3)_____.

Eric: Ryan, please don't _____(4)_____. It's really _____(5)_____. I'll just turn this knob right now and adjust the setting.

Ryan: In the future, please be sure to _____(6)_____.

Eric: No need to make a mountain out of a molehill. It's just one little mistake. Some people prefer extra spicy nacho chips anyway!

Ryan: It's not just one little mistake. Lately, your work hasn't been _____(7)_____. This may be a _____(8)_____, but several of us have noticed that your performance has been poor for the past six months.

ANSWERS TO LESSON 13, p. 192

Lesson 14

TAKING CREDIT FOR GOOD RESULTS

When United Supply Company launches their website three weeks ahead of schedule, there's more than one person ready to take credit.

Когда компания United Supply сумела открыть свой вэб-сайт на три недели раньше графика, в этом была заслуга не одного человека, а целого коллектива.

Bob: Kurt, I've got great news for you. We're **pushing the envelope** and *launching our new website* three weeks ahead of schedule.

Kurt: Wow, Bob, that's a first for this company! How did you **pull that off**?

Bob: I **burned the midnight oil** over these past few weeks. I **worked my tail off**. Sometimes things would get *tough*, but I always **kept my eye on the prize**.

Tara: Let's not forget about Jim in technical support. He really **hunkered down** these past few days, working **around the clock**.

Bob: Yeah, Jim's a real **team player.** He helped a lot.

Kurt: Well, that's not surprising. Jim's always ready to **pitch in**.

Bob: Of course, you deserve **a pat on the back** too, Kurt. None of this would've been possible without your leadership.

Kurt: **All in a day's work.** Providing great leadership **comes with the territory**. Well, time for some **R&R**. I'm off to Florida to play golf for a few days. See you next week!

IDIOMS & EXPRESSIONS – LESSON 14

(to) push the envelope – to go beyond what is normally done; to stretch the boundaries
приложить дополнительные усилия; превзойти ожидания; делать что-либо сверх нормы

➤ The design team **pushed the envelope** by creating a car powered entirely by the sun.

Происхождение. Это выражение пришло из программы летчиков-испытателей ВВС США 1940-х гг. Слово "envelope" означало предел технических возможностей самолета. Выходить за эти пределы было небезопасно. Том Вольф в своем бестселлере 1979 г. "The Right Stuff" о жизни летчиков-испытателей популяризировал идею "pushing the envelope" – выходить за пределы допустимого – и ввел это выражение в обиход.

(to) pull something off – to accomplish a difficult task; to successfully do something difficult
завершить трудную задачу; справиться с задачей; успешно реализовать сложное предприятие

➤ We need to prepare and mail out 50,000 media kits by tomorrow. I don't know how we're going to **pull it off**!

SYNONYM: to carry something off

(to) burn the midnight oil – to stay up late working or studying
работать или учиться допоздна; засиживаться за работой до глубокой ночи; полуночничать

➤ The bank needs our financial statements completed by 9 a.m. tomorrow. We're going to need to **burn the midnight oil** tonight to finish on time.

Происхождение. Это выражение восходит к эпохе до открытия электричества, когда для освещения использовались масляные лампы. В те времена люди ложились спать раньше, чем теперь. Если в лампе в полночь все еще горело масло, вы полуночничали, т.е. засиживались допоздна.

(to) work one's tail off – *see Lesson 11*

(to) keep one's eye on the prize – to stay focused on the end result; to not let small problems get in the way of good results
концентрироваться на главном; сосредоточиться на конечном результате; не дать незначительным проблемам быть помехой на пути к главной цели

➤ I know it's tough going to class after work, but just **keep your eye on the prize**. At the end of next year, you'll have your MBA.

Примечание. Возможно встретить как вариант: keep one's eyes on the prize.

(to) hunker down – to focus on work; to get ready to work hard, often involving a long period of time
уйти с головой в работу; надолго засесть за работу; не видеть белого света

➤ If you're going to finish that report by Monday morning, you'd better **hunker down** over the weekend.

Примечание. Эта фраза также может означать: «не выходить из помещения» или «найти убежище от непогоды». Например: We're expecting a blizzard tonight. We'd better just hunker down at home and not go anywhere.

---

around the clock – non-stop; 24 hours a day
без остановки; 24 часа в сутки; день и ночь

➤ When the company website went down, the IT department worked **around the clock** to fix it.

Примечание. Возможно встретить как вариант "round the clock".

---

team player – somebody willing to help out for the benefit of the group
командный игрок; тот, кто готов работать на благо коллектива

➤ Joe is great at working with others, and he always contributes a lot to projects. Everybody knows he's a **team player**!

(to) pitch in – to help; to contribute
помогать; вносить свою лепту

➤ If we're going to get these 3,000 crystal vases packaged and shipped by tomorrow morning, everybody's going to need to **pitch in**.

a pat on the back – *see Lesson 6*

all in a day's work – this is just part of the job; this is nothing unusual
это всего лишь работа; работа есть работа; это обычное дело

> "You've come up with a plan to double our sales next quarter?"
— "Yes, **all in a day's work**."

(to) come with the territory – to be part of the job
сопутствовать чему-либо; быть неотъемлемой частью работы

> Samantha doesn't like firing people, but as a vice president, she knows that **comes with the territory**.

R&R – rest and relaxation
отдыхать и расслабляться

> Brad and Melanie got plenty of **R&R** during their two-week vacation in the Caribbean.

✎ Practice the Idioms

Найдите наилучшую замену выделенным выражениям:

1) Your small company is trying to get distribution at Wal-Mart? How are you going to **pull that off?**
   a) succeed in doing that
   b) fail to do that
   c) compete with them

2) If you need help answering phones and taking orders, I'd be happy to **pitch in**.
   a) hang up on the customers
   b) help
   c) call

3) When you're the CEO of a tobacco company, dealing with lawsuits **comes with the territory**.
   a) is a great benefit
   b) is easily avoided
   c) is part of the job

84

4) If we're going to get all of these orders shipped in time for Christmas, we're going to have to **hunker down**!
   a) close for the holidays
   b) work really hard
   c) take it easy

5) During the negotiation, **keep your eye on the prize** and don't let the other side pressure you into a bad deal.
   a) watch the prize carefully
   b) stay focused on what's really important
   c) grab everything for yourself

6) You think consumers will be willing to pay $50,000 for a high-tech toilet? That's **pushing the envelope**.
   a) testing the limits of what people will pay
   b) a very reasonable price
   c) not something to be flushed down a toilet

7) You look exhausted. Why don't you take a few days off and **get some R&R**?
   a) spend some time relaxing
   b) take a trip by train
   c) work extra hours

8) If we want to submit the business plan by tomorrow afternoon, we're going to have to **burn the midnight oil** tonight.
   a) work until 7 p.m.
   b) relax
   c) work very late

ANSWERS TO LESSON 14, p. 192

Stop trying to pass the buck.

SHIFTING BLAME

Rick and Ellen work for Attic Treasures Antiques, an antique shop. Max is the owner of the shop. Recently, a woman came in and sold them $10,000 worth of "antique" jewelry. Max takes one look at the jewelry and realizes it's fake.

Рик и Эллен работают в антикварном магазине Attic Treasures Antiques. Макс – владелец магазина. На днях в магазине побывала женщина и продала его сотрудникам «старинные» украшения стоимостью в $10 000. Макс с первого взгляда определил, что ювелирные изделия – всего лишь подделка.

Max: I can't believe you two bought these fake antique necklaces! Didn't you examine them before **shelling out** 10 *grand?*

Rick: Yeah, I thought they were fake, but I let Ellen **talk me into** buying them.

Ellen: What? **I can't believe my ears!** You thought they were real. Now you're just trying to **cover yourself!**

Rick: I don't want to be the **fall guy** here, Ellen. You were the one who looked at them under a magnifying glass.

Ellen: **For the record**, you were the one **going on about** how you "**struck gold**" right after the woman left the shop!

Rick: I don't remember saying that. Stop trying to **pass the buck**. Just **step up to the plate** and admit your mistake!

Ellen: Right, while you **wash your hands of** the whole thing. **Dream on!**

IDIOMS & EXPRESSIONS – LESSON 15

(to) shell out – to pay (often more than one would like)
выложить; раскошелиться; переплатить за что-то втридорога

> The fast food chain had to **shell out** $10 million in a lawsuit after several people got sick from eating their hamburgers.

(to) talk someone into something – to convince someone to do something, often something that one later regrets
убедить, уговорить, подбить кого-либо на поступок, о котором впоследствии можно пожалеть

> Our president doesn't want to give us Christmas Eve off as a holiday. We're hoping our office manager can **talk him into** it.

I can't believe my ears! – I'm very surprised!
Что я слышу? Вот так новость! Я не верю своим ушам!

> Chris got fired? **I can't believe my ears!** He was one of our top salespeople!

(to) cover oneself – to try to avoid being blamed for something; to protect oneself from blame
подстраховаться; попытаться избежать ответственности за что-либо; обезопасить, прикрыть себя

> Nina knew her company was producing a defective product. She **covered herself** by keeping records of all of her letters and e-mails to her boss about the issue.

Примечание. Вам может также встретиться более грубая форма этого выражения: cover your ass, или краткий вариант "CYA".

fall guy – the person who gets blamed for a mistake, sometimes unfairly; scapegoat
мальчик для битья; всегда крайний; козёл отпущения; человек, которого незаслуженно обвиняют во всех грехах

> The company's entire management team wanted to enter the market in China. When the business failed there, they made Fred the **fall guy** and fired him.

for the record – *see Lesson 4*

(to) go on about – to talk too long about; to talk for a long time about (always said as a criticism); to brag
говорить о чем-либо долго и нудно (негативная окраска); долдонить; тянуть одну и ту же песню

➤ Bill is always **going on about** what a great salesman he is.

Synonym: to carry on about

(to) strike gold – to make a very profitable deal; to discover something valuable
напасть на золотую жилу; заключить очень выгодную сделку; найти что-то стоящее

➤ Christie **struck gold** with the idea of selling videos at discount prices on eBay.

(to) pass the buck – to shift the blame; to blame somebody else
переложить ответственность (на другого); сваливать вину на кого-то

➤ It's your fault. Don't try to **pass the buck**!

Происхождение. Это выражение пришло из карточной игры в покер, где "buck" означает: «фишка, указывающая кому сдавать в покере».

(to) step up to the plate – *see Lesson 4*

(to) wash one's hands of – to remove any association with; to stop being part of something; to refuse to take responsibility for
умыть руки; отмежеваться от чего-либо; снимать с себя ответственность

➤ When Molly realized her business partners were selling stolen goods, she decided to **wash her hands** of the whole business.

Происхождение. Это выражение взято из Библии. Понтий Пилат, римский наместник в Иудее, умыл руки перед толпой, отдав ей Иисуса для казни (имеется в виду ритуальное умывание рук, что свидетельствовало о непричастности к какому-либо событию).

Dream on! – That's what you'd like, but it's not realistic.
Размечтался! Не принимай желаемое за действительное!

➤ You want to retire in five years, and you've only got $5,000 in the bank? **Dream on!**

(to) point fingers at each other / (to) point the finger at someone
to blame
обвинять, упрекать; тыкать пальцем друг в друга / указывать пальцем на кого-либо

➤ Don't **point the finger at me**! You need to take the blame for this mistake.

(to) track something down – to find, usually with difficulty
выследить; отыскать, обычно с трудностями

➤ Natasha left an important file in a taxi, and now she's going to have to **track it down**.

✎ PRACTICE THE IDIOMS

Выберите наиболее подходящий ответ к каждому предложению:

1) Please don't try to talk me into exhibiting at your trade show.
   a) Okay, I'll sign you up.
   b) Okay, I'll call you tomorrow to talk about it some more.
   c) Okay, if you're sure you're not interested, I won't ask again.

2) I can't find Sam's address anywhere. Do you think you can help me track it down?
   a) Yes, I'd be happy to track it.
   b) Sure, I'll help you find it.
   c) No, but I'll help you find it.

3) We've already shelled out enough on advertising this year.
   a) I agree. Let's spend more.
   b) I know we've spent a lot, but I think we should do a couple more radio ads.
   c) I disagree. We've already spent a lot of money on advertising.

4) You think you'll be accepted to Harvard Business School? Dream on!
   a) You may not agree, but I think it's a realistic goal.
   b) Right, I'll just go to sleep and dream about it.
   c) Thanks for helping me think big.

5) I had nothing to do with the disastrous decision to hire Dennis. Don't point the finger at me!
   a) I'm not pointing the finger, but I *am* blaming you.
   b) Good. I'm glad you're willing to take the blame.
   c) Okay, I won't blame you.

6) I think we've struck gold with our idea to sell content on our website instead of giving it away for free. What do you think?
   a) I agree. It's a great idea.
   b) I agree. Nobody's going to be willing to pay for it.
   c) I agree. We should sell silver and bronze on the site too.

7) You need to take responsibility for our accounting problems. Stop trying to pass the buck!
   a) Okay, I won't pass it anymore. You can have it.
   b) I already passed the buck.
   c) I'm not trying to pass the buck. I admit I made a mistake.

8) You finally got promoted, and now you're leaving your company and opening a health food store? I can't believe my ears!
   a) Yes, I know it's a surprising move.
   b) I couldn't believe my ears either.
   c) I know you're not surprised.

ANSWERS TO LESSON 15, p. 192

REVIEW FOR LESSONS 11-15

Вставьте пропущенные слова:

1) Brent has an opinion about everything. No matter what the topic is, he has to put in his _____ cents.

   a) ten   b) five   c) two

2) I can't believe that Katrina forgot to order sandwiches for our lunch meeting. She really _____ the ball!

   a) left   b) dropped   c) forgot

3) Sales are down by 30 percent so far this year. Let's think of some ways we can turn _____ the business.

   a) up   b) about   c) around

4) Our copy machine is broken. Before we shell _____ for a new one, let's call the repairman and see if he can fix it.

   a) out   b) up   c) about

5) The pharmaceutical company spent millions of dollars trying to come up with a cure for cancer, before finally deciding to throw _____ the towel.

   a) out   b) up   c) in

6) I won't go over all the details in the contract with you now, but _____ a nutshell, we are offering to pay you $150,000 a year for your services.

   a) by   b) in   c) with

7) Joan's letters to clients often have typos in them. In the future, she should _____ her i's and _____ her t's.

   a) cross...dot   b) dot...cross   c) label...watch

8) We're going to _____ the envelope and try a brand new type of online advertising this year.

   a) push   b) pull   c) address

9) One of our customers is looking for a humidifier that also works as an air filter. Can you help her track that _____?

   a) down   b) up   c) out

10) You need to speak with Brandon about his performance. Lately, it hasn't been _____ to scratch.

   a) down   b) about   c) up

11) Since he made the big sale two years ago, Mike hasn't worked very hard. He's been _____ on his laurels.

   a) resting   b) sleeping   c) relying

12) Before we make a final decision, does anybody else want to weigh _____ on this issue?

   a) out   b) in   c) about

13) Don't try to pass the _____ to your employees. It's time you take some responsibility.

   a) buck   b) dollar   c) responsibility

14) We've got to call 200 customers as part of our market research survey. Who's going to pitch _____ and start making calls?

   a) out   b) up   c) in

15) If we get _____ track, we're not going to be able to finish our meeting on time.

   a) on   b) around   c) off

ANSWERS TO REVIEW, p. 193

We need to do some belt-tightening.

POLITELY DISAGREEING
WITH SOMEONE

If Kroll Enterprises doesn't take action soon, the company is going to be in financial trouble. Joel and Kathy have different opinions on how to cut costs at the company.

Фирме Kroll Enterprises придется столкнуться с финансовыми трудностями, если срочно не будут приняты надлежащие меры. Джоэл и Кэти расходятся во мнениях о том, как сократить расходы компании.

Kathy: We're going to be **in the red** again this year.

Joel: I think we should **cut back on** employee health benefits. We could **save a bundle**.

Kathy: True, it might help the **bottom line**, but our employees would be really unhappy. I would only recommend it as a **last resort**.

Joel: Well, we need to do some **belt-tightening**. We can either have a *salary freeze* or we can cut back on their health benefits. I think I've chosen **the lesser of two evils**.

Kathy: Another *salary freeze* is **out of the question**. All our best employees will quit.

Joel: I'm caught **between a rock and a hard place**. I have to cut costs.

Kathy: Do you really? I don't think cutting costs is **the name of the game**. I think the secret is figuring out how to increase our sales.

Joel: How do you suggest we **pull that off**?

Kathy: Let's meet with the other vice presidents and **bat around some ideas**.

Joel: We can talk **until we're blue in the face**. We need to take action now.

Kathy: It's clear that you and I **don't see eye-to-eye**. For now, **let's just agree to disagree**.

IDIOMS & EXPRESSIONS – LESSON 16

in the red – *see Lesson 2*

(to) cut back on – to reduce
снизить; уменьшить; сократить; урезать

➤ We need to save money by **cutting back on** business travel. Please conduct most of your meetings by videoconference from now on.

(to) save a bundle – to save a lot of money
сэкономить кучу денег

➤ By outsourcing their call center operations to India, the credit card company **saved a bundle**.

---

bottom line – эта идиома имеет 2 значения:
1) profits; financial results
прибыль; финансовые результаты

➤ Falling prices for televisions and other electronic equipment have hurt Sony's **bottom line**.

2) the final result; the main point
итог; конечный результат

➤ The **bottom line** is that your company is not big enough to supply us with all of the packaging we need.

Происхождение. В бухгалтерском учете итоговая линия показывает чистый приход (прибыль за вычетом всех расходов). Это главный показатель прибыльности бизнеса.

last resort – if there are no other alternatives left; the last solution for getting out of a difficulty
крайняя мера в безвыходной ситуации; единственное решение для выхода из трудного положения

➤ There must be some way to create more demand for our products. We should only lower our prices as a **last resort**.

---

belt-tightening – reduction of expenses
затянуть потуже пояс; перейти в режим экономии; вынужденное сокращение расходов

➤ When worldwide demand for software decreased, Microsoft had to do some **belt-tightening**.

---

the lesser of two evils – when you have two unattractive options and you choose the one that is better; the better of two bad options
выбрать меньшее из двух зол

➤ Both shuttle services offering rides to the airport are bad. You'll just have to choose **the lesser of two evils**.

---

out of the question – impossible
об этом не может быть и речи; это исключено; это невозможно

➤ We couldn't possibly afford to open an office in Europe right now. It's **out of the question**.

---

between a rock and a hard place – in a very difficult position; facing two choices which are equally unacceptable or difficult
между молотом и наковальней; между двух огней; в затруднительном положении

➤ I wish I could offer you a better discount, but my boss would be angry. I'm caught **between a rock and a hard place**.

---

the name of the game – the central issue; the most important thing; the main goal
суть дела, самое главное; основная цель; досл.: «название игры»

➤ If we're going to operate more effectively, better communication is **the name of the game**.

(to) pull something off – *see Lesson 14*

(to) bat around some ideas – to discuss ideas; to discuss options
обсуждать идеи; прикидывать варианты; обмениваться мнениями

> We need to come up with a creative marketing plan. Let's meet on Monday morning to **bat around some ideas**.

until one is blue in the face – for a very long time, with no results
до посинения; долго, но без результатов

> You can argue with the customer service people **until you're blue in the face**, but they won't give you your money back.

(to) not see eye-to-eye – *see Lesson 12*

let's just agree to disagree – we don't agree, but let's not argue any further; let's accept our differences of opinion and move on
наши мнения не совпадают, но давайте прекратим дальнейшие споры; давайте сойдемся на том, что наши мнения расходятся по каким-то вопросам и пойдем дальше

> I don't want to get in a fight with you about this. **Let's just agree to disagree**.

☙ PRACTICE THE IDIOMS

Найдите наилучшую замену выделенным выражениям:

1) I know we need to **do some belt-tightening**, but I'm not sure that laying off employees is the solution.
   a) increase our revenues
   b) get rid of some people
   c) reduce our expenses

2) Changing the packaging design at this point is **out of the question**. We're already in production.
   a) not a possibility
   b) a good idea
   c) probably not possible

3) If we're serious about saving money, we should consider **cutting back on** our use of expensive consultants.
   a) eliminating
   b) reducing
   c) increasing

4) You can tell me about how great Jim is **until you're blue in the face**. The fact is, I don't like the way he does business.
   a) until your face turns blue
   b) all you want
   c) until I change my mind

5) Kyle and Mark are meeting at Flanagan's Bar after work to **bat around some ideas about starting their own business**.
   a) discuss ideas about starting their own business
   b) dismiss the idea of starting their own business
   c) finalize plans to start their own bar

6) When you're the boss, demonstrating great leadership is **the name of the game**.
   a) not important
   b) somewhat important
   c) very important

7) The food manufacturer's costs have gone up, but they are unable to raise the price of their products. They're **caught between a rock and a hard place**.
   a) stuck in an undesirable position
   b) ready to go out of business
   c) deciding between two great options

8) Why don't you open a corporate account with DHL and ship all of your packages with them? **You could save a bundle**.
   a) You could stop carrying heavy packages.
   b) You could save a few dollars.
   c) You could save a lot of money.

ANSWERS TO LESSON 16, p. 193

Shape up or ship out!

TELLING SOMEBODY OFF* - Part 1

Doug and Joe work at the reception desk of the Boston Empire Hotel, a large hotel. Kara, the hotel manager, yells at Doug for being late to work every day.

Дуг и Джо работают в службе размещения крупной гостиницы Boston Empire Hotel. Кара, менеджер отеля, отчитывает Дуга за то, что он ежедневно опаздывает на работу.

Doug: Good morning, guys. How's it going?

Joe: Lousy. You were supposed to be here at 8 a.m. It's now 11 o'clock. **What's the deal?**

Doug: Sorry about that. My alarm didn't go off this morning.

Kara: You've been late every day this week!

Doug: I **had a rough night** last night. My girlfriend Liz **dumped me** and told me she's in love with my best friend!

Kara: Oh please, **spare us the sob story**!

Joe: I'm **sick and tired of** your excuses. You need to start **pulling your weight** around here.

Doug: Hey, **cut me some slack**! My life is a mess right now.

Kara: Doug, I'm trying to **run a tight ship**. I can't continue **turning a blind eye** to the fact that you're always late. **Shape up or ship out!**

Doug: I promise tomorrow I'll be here at 8 a.m. **on the dot**.

* отчитывать кого-либо

IDIOMS & EXPRESSIONS – LESSON 17
Part I

What's the deal? – What's going on? What happened? What's the explanation?
В чем дело? Что происходит?

➤ We received 5,000 mailing envelopes from your company, and you sent us an invoice for 50,000. **What's the deal?**

(to) have a rough night – to have a difficult evening or night
плохо провести вечер или ночь; провести бурную ночь

➤ You look exhausted this morning. Did you **have a rough night**?

(to) dump someone – to end a romantic relationship; to break up with someone
порвать близкие взаимоотношения; бросить кого-либо

➤ Walter Jenkins, the CEO of a real estate firm, **dumped** his wife of 40 years and married his young assistant.

---

spare us *(or me)* **the sob story** – don't bother making excuses; don't try to explain yourself
избавь нас от душещипательных историй; не нужно оправданий или объяснений

➤ You can't finish your work tonight because you've got a toothache? **Spare me the sob story**!

Примечание. Слово "sob" означает «рыдать навзрыд, всхлипывать».

---

sick and tired of – completely bored with; sick of; fed up with
до смерти надоело; быть по горло сытым

➤ Jane is **sick and tired of** dealing with her nasty boss. She's looking forward to quitting her job next month.

(to) pull one's weight – to do one's share of the work
внести свою лепту

➤ So far, you haven't contributed much to this project. Please start **pulling your weight**.

Примечание. Встречается также вариант — to pull one's own weight.

(to) cut someone some slack – to be forgiving; to not judge someone too harshly
быть снисходительным; давать поблажку; не судить слишком строго

➤ **Cut Gretchen some slack** for failing to finish the report on time. She's going through a bitter divorce.

(to) run a tight ship – to run something effectively and efficiently
эффективно управлять чем-либо; быть на плаву; вести непотопляемый корабль

➤ Jack Welch is known as one of the greatest business leaders ever. He **ran a tight ship** while he was the CEO of General Electric.

(to) turn a blind eye to something – to ignore a problem or an issue; to refuse to recognize
закрывать на что-либо глаза; игнорировать существование проблемы; не обращать внимания

➤ Every September when the school year starts, pens and paper disappear from our company's supply room. We can no longer **turn a blind eye to this**.

Shape up or ship out! – improve your behavior or leave; if you don't improve your performance, you're going to get fired
берись за ум или уходи; вы должны изменить свое поведение или уйти; если вы не изменитесь к лучшему, вы будете уволены

➤ Martin finally had enough of Todd's negative attitude. "**Shape up or ship out!**" he told Todd.

Происхождение. Это выражение появилось в лексиконе военнослужащих США во время Второй мировой войны и употреблялось в следующем значении: вам следует подчиняться уставу и вести себя как положено; в противном случае мы будем вынуждены послать вас в зону военных действий за океан – «ship out».

---

on the dot – sharp; at an exact time
минута в минуту; точно; строго в назначенное время

➤ The videoconference with our Tokyo office will start at 10 a.m. **on the dot**.

Telling Somebody Off, Part 2: The Next Day...

Doug: Sorry, I'm **running behind**. I had to…

Kara: **Don't waste your breath**! You're three hours late again.

Doug: But my car wouldn't start, my mechanic is on vacation in Florida, and then I…

Kara: Today was **the last straw**. You're fired!

Doug: That's fine. I was miserable working for a **slave driver** like you anyway!

Kara: **Don't burn your bridges**. You may need me later as a *reference*.

IDIOMS & EXPRESSIONS – LESSON 17 Part 2

(to be) running behind – to be late; to be delayed
опаздывать; задерживаться

➤ I'm calling to say I'm **running behind**. I'll be at your office in 15 minutes.

SYNONYM: running late

---

don't waste your breath – don't bother; don't bother trying to defend yourself; I don't want to hear your excuses
не трать попусту слова; не ищи оправданий; я не хочу слушать твои отговорки

➤ **Don't waste your breath** trying to talk me into buying an advertisement in your magazine. I've already spent my advertising budget for the year.

(the) last straw – the final offense or annoyance that pushes one to take action
последняя капля, переполнившая чашу чьего-либо терпения

➤ First you tell me I can't have an office and now you're cutting my salary. This is **the last straw**. I quit!

Происхождение. Эта поговорка произошла от другого выражения, с которым, возможно, вам приходилось сталкиваться: соломинка, переломившая спину верблюду. Известно, что одна соломинка ничего не весит. Но если навьючивают на верблюда много соломы, может наступить момент, когда груз станет настолько тяжелым, что одна соломинка сломает верблюду спину. Так и люди могут мириться до поры до времени с небольшими неудобствами или неприятностями. Но когда их накапливается слишком много, людям это надоедает, и они переходят к действию.

---

slave driver – a very demanding and often cruel boss or supervisor
слишком требовательный и часто жестокий, безжалостный начальник; надсмотрщик; эксплуататор

➤ You're going to be working late hours as an assistant brand manager in Linda's group. She's a real **slave driver**!

Происхождение. Во времена рабства так называли человека, который наблюдал за невольниками на плантациях.

(to) burn one's bridges – to do something which makes it impossible to go back; to damage a relationship to such an extent that one can never go back to that person again
сжигать за собой мосты; сделать что-то такое, что делает невозможным возвращение назад; испортить взаимоотношения с кем-либо до такой степени, что примирение исключено

➤ When he was fired, Chad really felt like telling Lisa that she was a terrible manager, but he didn't want to **burn his bridges**.

Происхождение. Это выражение пришло из военного лексикона. Во времена Римской Империи солдаты имели обыкновение сжигать за собой мосты, отрезая себе дорогу к отступлению, что укрепляло их волю к победе.

✎ PRACTICE THE IDIOMS

Заполните пропуски, используя следующие идиомы:

slave driver	the last straw
shape up or ship out	run a tight ship
turn a blind eye	What's the deal?
cut me some slack	pulling his weight
sick and tired	spare me the sob story

Jill is a manager of the automotive department at Sears. One of her salespeople, Len, isn't ___(1)___ . Jill is ___(2)___ of the fact that Len shows up late every day and is constantly flirting with Tatiana, the saleswoman in the electronics department. Yesterday, Jill watched as Len was rude to a customer. "Go get your tires somewhere else!" Len yelled at the customer. That was ___(3)___ . She pulled him aside and said to him, "Len, ___(4)___ !" Len was surprised. "___(5)___ " he asked. "I thought you and I were friends, and now suddenly you're turning into a ___(6)___ ." Jill replied, "Len, I do like you, but I'm trying to ___(7)___ here. I can no longer ___(8)___ to the fact that you're not taking this job very seriously." Len turned red and frowned. "Hey, ___(9)___ . I've been under a lot of stress lately at home." Jill didn't want to hear any excuses. "___(10)___ ," she replied.

ANSWERS TO LESSON 17, p. 193

DISCUSSING OFFICE SCANDALS

With his naughty behavior, Bill Swing provides plenty of material for office gossip. Cindy and Steve discuss his latest move and review his other recent insensitive behavior.

Своим беспутным поведением Билл Свинг дает достаточно поводов для сплетен в офисе. Синди и Стив обсуждают его последнюю выходку и судачат о его недавних похождениях.

Cindy: Did you hear **the latest dirt**?

Steve: Of course not. I'm totally **out of the loop**! I'm always the last one to find out everything.

Cindy: **According to the rumor mill**, Bill Swing **made a pass at** Laura Teller, the new marketing manager. Now she's threatening to sue him for *sexual harassment*.

Steve: Sounds like Bill's **up to his old tricks** again. He's always **on the make**. Last year, Paula Reynolds accused him of pinching her...

Cindy: I remember that. Too bad Paula quit before they could **get to the bottom of it**.

Steve: Two years ago he **got nailed** for organizing a *company offsite* to a *strip joint!*

Cindy: Oh, that really **takes the cake**. That's so **un-PC**!

Steve: Bill is definitely *not* **politically correct**!

Cindy: **What goes around comes around**. One day, **he'll get his**.

IDIOMS & EXPRESSIONS – LESSON 18

the latest dirt – the latest gossip
последняя сплетня

> Have you heard **the latest dirt**? Rob was fired for calling the chairman of the board a "jerk" to his face.

out of the loop – unaware of what's going on
не иметь понятия о том, что происходит

> If you want to know what's really going on at the company, don't bother asking Adam. He's **out of the loop**.

according to the rumor mill – according to gossip
если верить сплетням; согласно слухам

> **According to the rumor mill**, Randall didn't leave his position voluntarily. He was fired.

(to) make a pass at someone – to make a sexual advance toward someone
делать попытки ухаживать; домогаться кого-либо

> Glen got drunk at the office holiday party and **made a pass at** Sara, his secretary. Unfortunately for Glen, Sara's husband was in the same room!

up to one's old tricks – repeating the same behavior as before (usually annoying, dishonest, or sneaky behavior)
повторять свои старые трюки; взяться за старое (обычно о недостойном поведении, обмане, подлости)

> Our boss is **up to his old tricks**. This is the third time we've gone out to lunch and he's forgotten his wallet back at the office.

on the make – эта идиома имеет 2 значения:

1) actively looking for a sexual partner
активно искать сексуального партнера

> Look at Ron flirting with our new receptionist! He's always **on the make**.

2) aggressively trying to improve one's social or financial status
изо всех сил пытаться поднять свой социальный или финансовый статус

> Jeff works 80-hour weeks as an investment banker in Manhattan. He's as an ambitious young man **on the make**.

get to the bottom of something – *see Lesson 7*

(to) get nailed – to get in trouble; to get caught doing something
попасться на чем-то (с поличным); быть припертым к стене

> Troy tried to cheat on his expense report by including a dinner he had with his girlfriend, but he **got nailed** and had to return the money.

(to) take the cake – to rank first; to be the best or worst example of something
получить приз; быть первым во всем – и в хорошем, и в плохом

> Bob stole your idea and presented it as his own during the meeting? That really **takes the cake**!

Происхождение. В Древней Греции торт являлся популярным призом, которым награждали победителей.

un-PC – insensitive; offensive; not politically correct (PC)
нетактичный; агрессивный; оскорбительный; не политкоррект-ный; досл.: не совпадающий с государственной или полити-ческой точкой зрения

> George came right out and asked his colleague if he was gay? That's so **un-PC**!

politically correct (PC) – это выражение относится к речи или поведению, которые тщательно контролируются (иногда черес-чур), чтобы не оскорбить окружающих в вопросах сексуальной, расовой, религиозной принадлежности и т.д. Эта концепция возникла в 1980 гг. в США. В наши дни это выражение получило негативную окраску.

> The university president suggested that women may not be as good at men in science because of differences in their brains? That's not **politically correct**!

what goes around comes around – people usually get what they deserve in the end
как аукнется, так и откликнется; что посеешь, то пожнешь; люди обычно получают то, что заслуживают

> Dana is always trying to steal everybody else's clients. But **what goes around comes around**.

he'll get his / she'll get hers – something bad will happen to him (or her), just as he (or she) deserves
он/она свое еще получит; с ним/с ней обязательно что-то случится; он/она получит по заслугам

> Beth got promoted to vice president after firing half her staff? Don't worry, **she'll get hers**.

SYNONYM: he (or she) will get what's coming to him (or her)

✎ PRACTICE THE IDIOMS

Найдите наилучшую замену выделенным словам:

1) Jake says he only hires pretty girls to work at his restaurant. He's so **un-PC!**
   a) bad with computers
   b) kind
   c) offensive

2) Tiffany called in sick on Tuesday, and she showed up for work on Wednesday with a suntan. She's going to **get nailed** for lying about being sick.
   a) be awarded
   b) get in trouble
   c) get fired

3) Brad said that Tammy **made a pass at him** while they were on a business trip in Moscow.
   a) tried to initiate a sexual relationship with him
   b) threw a football at him
   c) was rude to him

4) Frank keeps taking all of the best customer accounts for himself. We hope that one of these days, **he'll get his**.
   a) he'll get his own accounts
   b) something bad will happen to him
   c) he'll actually earn the accounts he's taking

5) I'm not surprised that Randy kept trying to put his arm around you during the business dinner. He's always **on the make**.
   a) affectionate in public
   b) looking for romance
   c) moving quickly

6) Our CEO was one of the last people to hear of the accounting scandal at our company. He's so **out of the loop!**
   a) aware of what's going on
   b) unaware of what's going on
   c) curious about what's going on

7) Monica loves to gossip, so you can always count on her for the **latest dirt**.
   a) most up-to-date gossip
   b) news of important current events
   c) nastiest rumors

8) Three months after he laid off thousands of employees on Christmas Eve, the CEO himself was fired. **What goes around comes around.**
   a) When you fire somebody, you'll probably get fired yourself soon.
   b) The CEO will still come around the offices.
   c) When people do bad things, they're usually punished in the end.

ANSWERS TO LESSON 18, p. 193

He gave me an earful.

COMPLAINING ABOUT A CO-WORKER

Justin, from the marketing department, is complaining to Mary about Joe. Joe is always nasty to Justin and Justin is sick of it. Mary advises Justin not to let Joe bother him.

Джастин из отдела по маркетингу жалуется Мэри на Джо. Джо всегда ведет себя злобно и вызывающе по отношению к Джастину, и тому надоело это терпеть. Мэри советует Джастину не разрешать Джо донимать себя.

Mary: How did the meeting with Joe go?

Justin: Lousy. He was **in a snit**.

Mary: Why?

Justin: He **got bent out of shape** over the fact that I didn't bring him the sales *forecasts*. He **gave me an earful** about how people from the marketing department never bring him the right information.

Mary: Don't worry about him. Don't let him **push your buttons**.

Justin: I'll just have to **steer clear of him** now that I know he's such a **hot-head**.

Mary: He's **not a bad guy**, but **he does have issues**. And he's **got a chip on his shoulder** when it comes to marketing people.

Justin: Joe's always **on his high horse** about something.

Mary: You'll just have to **grin and bear it**. We've got a lot of personalities around here.* You'll just have to learn to work with them.

Justin: Well, I don't know how I'm going to be able to work with him. He **gets under my skin**.

* Это вежливый способ выразить примерно следующее: Многие люди, работающие здесь, очень странные, и с ними тяжело работать.

IDIOMS & EXPRESSIONS – LESSON 19

in a snit – in a bad mood; angry
в плохом настроении; раздражительный

➤ No wonder Donna's **in a snit**. She just found out she didn't get the promotion she was expecting.

(to be or to get) bent out of shape – to be or to get very angry about something
выйти из себя из-за чего-либо; рассердиться

➤ When Nick's boss told him he couldn't take two weeks off for a vacation, he **got bent out of shape**.

(to) give somebody an earful – to say what one really thinks, in detail
устроить кому-либо нагоняй, взбучку, разнос; высказать все, что думаешь (обычно, критические замечания, которые могут быть неприятны тому, к кому они относятся)

➤ When Leo showed up late for work, his boss **gave him an earful**.

(to) push one's buttons – to annoy someone; to make someone angry
докучать, надоедать кому-либо; раздражать кого-либо

➤ Liz **pushes my buttons** with her bossy behavior.

(to) steer clear of somebody or something – to avoid or stay away from someone or something
избегать кого-либо, что-либо; держаться подальше, в стороне

➤ Ray is on a low-carb diet. He needs to **steer clear of** bread and pasta and other foods high in carbohydrates.

---

hot-head – a bad tempered or very moody person; a violent person
горячий, вспыльчивый; сумасброд, неуравновешенный, невоспитанный; человек настроения

➤ Don't feel bad that Tim yelled at you. He's a real **hot-head**, and he yells at people all the time.

---

not a bad guy – an okay person
в общем неплохой человек (обычно, когда вам не очень нравятся отдельные черты характера в человеке, но в целом вы к нему неплохо относитесь)

➤ Tim does have a bad temper, but he's **not a bad guy**.

(to) have (some) issues – to have some personality problems
иметь проблемы личностного характера (один из способов намекнуть на чьи-либо непривлекательные черты характера)

➤ Elizabeth can be difficult to work with. She **has some issues**.

(to) have a chip on one's shoulder – to remain angry about a past insult; to bear a grudge
быть готовым к драке; искать повод к ссоре; держаться вызывающе

➤ Ever since Mike was told he had to leave his office and move into a cubicle, he's **had a chip on his shoulder**.

Происхождение. Это выражение пришло из американской лексики 19 века. Когда кто-то искал повод начать драку, он клал на плечо щепку и провоцировал своего оппонента сбить ее. Хотя этот обычай больше не существует, мы продолжаем говорить, что раздраженный человек «has a chip on his shoulder».

(to be or to get) on one's high horse – to have an arrogant or superior attitude; to think one has all the answers
важничать; высокомерно вести себя; относиться к другим свысока

➤ Hank's **on his high horse** again, telling everybody around him how to behave.

Примечание. Вы можете услышать производные выражения: "Get off your high horse!", что означает «Перестань высокомерничать!» (досл.: «Слезай с коня!»).

(to) grin and bear it – to put up with it; to pretend it doesn't bother you
скрывать под улыбкой свои переживания; делать вид, что все в порядке; не подавать виду; терпеть, стиснув зубы

➤ I know you don't like traveling with your boss, but it'll just be a short trip. Just **grin and bear it**.

Примечание. "Grin" имеет значение «улыбаться»; "bear" означает «терпеливо сносить».

(to) get under one's skin – to bother; to irritate; to annoy
докучать, надоедать; действовать на нервы; лезть в душу

➤ Your boss is annoying, but don't let him **get under your skin**!

✎ Practice the Idioms

Заполните пропуски, используя следующие идиомы:

issues with her	**get bent out of shape**
gets under his skin	**hot-head**
grin and bear it	**in a snit**
push my buttons	**steer clear**

Tracy has a reputation for having a bad temper. Everybody in the office knows she is a ___(1)___ . When she's in a bad mood, it's best to just ___(2)___ of her. Seth doesn't like Tracy. He has ___(3)___ . He complained to their boss, Yuri, about how much she ___(4)___ . "Too bad," said Yuri. "You have to work with her even though you don't like her, so just ___(5)___ ."

Today, Seth went into Tracy's office and asked her to help him gather some sales data. "Why should I?" asked Tracy. Seth replied, "Why are you ___(6)___ ? This is a simple task. There's no need to ___(7)___ just because I'm asking for your help." Tracy got angry, pounded her fist on her desk, and yelled, "Seth, you really know how to ___(8)___ ! I'm sick and tired of doing *your* job all the time. If you want sales data, get it yourself!"

ANSWERS TO LESSON 19, p. 193

TALKING ABOUT A BROWN NOSER
Part 1

Nearly every office has one: the brown noser. He or she will do just about anything to win favor with the boss. Here Tony, Karen, and Nancy complain about their local brown noser, Mitch.

Почти в каждом офисе есть такой человек, который повсюду сует свой нос. Он или она сделают все, чтобы угодить боссу. Тони, Карен и Нэнси жалуются на своего «штатного» подхалима Митча.

Tony: I was just in a meeting with Mitch and Bill. Mitch said to Bill, "Bill, we're so lucky to have you as our boss. You're such a great leader!"

Karen: He's **up to his old tricks**. He was trying to earn **brownie points** with Bill.

Nancy: Mitch has the reputation of being a **yes man** and a **brown noser**. He's an expert at **kissing up**.

Tony: Then he said to Bill, "Other people here don't appreciate you like I do!" **Talk about** trying to **butter up** the boss!

Nancy: Yeah, and this time **at our expense**! He's just **out for himself**.

Karen: Well, it's a **dog-eat-dog world**. Obviously he thinks this is the way to **get ahead**.

Tony: I guess it's one way to **climb the corporate ladder**. But I could never **look at myself in the mirror** after behaving that way.

Karen: I'm not good at **kissing up** either. **No wonder** I've been in the same lousy position for 10 years!

IDIOMS & EXPRESSIONS – LESSON 20
Part 1

up to one's old tricks – *see Lesson 18*

---

brownie points – credit for doing a good deed or for giving someone a compliment (usually a boss or teacher)
зачет за доброе дело; скаутское очко; знак одобрения, стимул; здесь в значении: делать вещи в угоду кому-то (обычно начальнику или учителю)

➤ Sara scored **brownie points** with her boss by volunteering to organize the company's holiday party.

Происхождение. Девочек-скаутов младшего возраста называют Brownies ("брауни" – «шоколадное печенье»). После каждого доброго дела им зачитывается очко. Набрав определенное количество очков, девочки получают значки за отличие. Когда это выражение относится к взрослым, оно приобретает ироническую окраску.

---

yes man – an employee who always agrees with the boss or does whatever the boss says
работник, который всегда согласен с начальством и готов сделать все, о чем бы его ни попросил босс

➤ Don't expect Tony to argue with the boss. He's a **yes man**.

---

brown noser – somebody who's always trying to win favor with those in authority, like bosses or teachers
подхалим, льстец; человек, который всегда пытается завоевать расположение начальства или учителей

➤ Jim told Amanda she was the best boss he ever had? What a **brown noser**!

Примечание. Есть также глагольная форма от "to brown nose."

(to) kiss up to (someone) – to try to win favor with someone by flattering them
льстить в корыстных целях; беззастенчиво угождать кому-либо; лизоблюдствовать

➤ Martin is always **kissing up to** the boss. He'll probably get promoted soon.

talk about – that's an example of…
вот пример (чего-либо)

> Sharon told everybody that Carla was having an affair with her boss. **Talk about** spreading nasty rumors!

(to) butter up – to say nice things to somebody, hoping that they'll do something nice for you in the future; to compliment too much
умасливать кого-либо; петь дифирамбы, засыпать комплиментами кого-либо в надежде на благосклонность в будущем

> Sam is trying to get promoted by **buttering up** his boss. His co-workers don't like his behavior.

at one's expense – at a cost to
за чей-то счет

> If you blame the project failure on us, you'll look better, but **at our expense**.

Примечание. Употребляется также выражение "at one's own expense" – «за свой собственный счет»: Joe wanted the job so badly, he was willing to fly to Atlanta for the interview at his own expense.

out for oneself – selfish; just concerned with oneself and one's own success; not caring about what happens to other people
эгоист; тот, кто думает только о своем успехе, не заботясь об окружающих

> I'm not surprised that Jessica took all the credit for the success of the ad campaign. She's just **out for herself**.

dog-eat-dog world – a cruel and aggressive world in which people just look out for themselves
жестокий, беспощадный мир бизнеса, живущий по принципу «каждый за себя», «человек человеку волк»

> Your company fired you shortly after you had a heart attack? Well, it's certainly a **dog-eat-dog world**!

Примечание. Это выражение восходит к 15-16 вв. В те времена частыми были сцены, когда дикие собаки насмерть дрались из-за куска пищи чтобы выжить. Была проведена ассоциация с людьми, которые готовы «перегрызть друг другу глотку» за свои интересы.

(to) get ahead – to get promoted; to advance in one's career
преуспеть; добиться успеха; продвинуться по службе

> If you want to **get ahead** in investment banking, be prepared to work long hours!

(to) climb the corporate ladder – advance in one's career; the process of getting promoted and making it to senior management
подняться по служебной лестнице; получить повышение и выбиться в начальники

> You want to **climb the corporate ladder**? It helps to be productive and to look good in front of your boss.

(to) look at oneself in the mirror – to face oneself
посмотреть на себя в зеркало (здесь в значении: стыдно «поднять глаза»)

> After firing so many employees, I don't know how Beth can even **look at herself in the mirror**.

no wonder – *see Lesson 7*

Talking About a Brown Noser, Part 2: When You're Overheard

Mitch: Hey guys. Don't you know it's rude to **talk behind someone's back**? I just overheard your entire conversation!

Tony: Sorry, Mitch. We didn't mean to offend you.

Mitch: Well, **the walls have ears**. **Think twice** before you insult me again!

Nancy: **Chill out!** We were talking about a different Mitch, not you.

Tony: That's right. We were talking about Mitch Schneider, over in the accounting department.

Mitch: **Likely story. I wasn't born yesterday!**

120

(to) talk behind someone's back – to gossip about somebody; to say negative things about somebody who's not around

сплетничать, распускать слухи, говорить о ком-либо плохо за глаза, за спиной

➤ Please don't **talk behind my back**. If you have something to say to me, say it to my face.

---

the walls have ears – you never know when somebody might be listening to your "private" conversation

и стены имеют уши; всегда может найтись кто-то, кто может подслушать или случайно услышать частный разговор

➤ Don't complain about the boss while we're in the office. Remember, **the walls have ears**!

(to) think twice – to think more carefully before doing something in the future; to not repeat a mistake one has made

подумать дважды, прежде чем сделать что-либо; не повторять прошлые ошибки

➤ Jane didn't even thank you for your Christmas gift? You should **think twice** before giving her a gift next year!

Chill out! – Relax! Don't worry!
Остынь! Успокойся! Не стоит беспокоиться!

➤ **Chill out!** Your presentation to the CEO will go fine.

---

likely story – that's not true; I find that hard to believe
Ну, конечно! Рассказывай! Так я в это и поверил! (ироническое замечание, когда история не выглядит правдоподобной)

➤ When Jim and Jenny were caught kissing in the conference room, they said it would never happen again. That's a **likely story**!

I wasn't born yesterday! – I'm not stupid; I'm not naive
Я не вчера родился! Нашли простака! Не на того напали!

➤ I just got an e-mail from a Nigerian company promising to send me $10 million next year if I send them $10,000 now. Too bad for them **I wasn't born yesterday!**

🖎 Practice the Idioms

Выберите наиболее подходящий ответ к каждому предложению:

1) We'd better be careful what we say in the office.
   a) That's right. The walls have ears.
   b) Likely story!
   c) Right, I wasn't born yesterday.

2) Eric, we're going to have to ask you to take a 40 percent pay cut. But next year, I promise we'll triple your salary.
   a) Lower your voice. The walls have ears!
   b) Don't get too excited. Chill out!
   c) That's hard to believe. I wasn't born yesterday!

3) Jill is constantly flattering her boss and offering to do favors for him.
   a) Why doesn't she butter him up instead?
   b) Think twice before accepting favors from her.
   c) That's one way to climb the corporate ladder.

4) I'm giving a presentation to our CEO in a half an hour. I'm so nervous!
   a) Likely story.
   b) Chill out!
   c) You're such a yes man.

5) I spent three hours helping Bob with his financial projections, and he didn't even say thank you.
   a) You need to look at yourself in the mirror.
   b) I'm sure you'll think twice before helping him again.
   c) He's trying to climb the corporate ladder.

6) Maria works at least 60 hours a week at the law firm and always volunteers for extra work. She's an excellent employee.
   a) She'll definitely get ahead.
   b) Let's not talk about her behind her back.
   c) It's a dog-eat-dog world.

122

7) Paul was arrested for stealing millions of dollars from his company.
    a) I'm not surprised. He's a real yes man.
    b) That's one way to climb the corporate ladder.
    c) I don't know how he can look at himself in the mirror.

8) You're the best boss I've ever had and definitely the smartest!
    a) Are you just out for yourself?
    b) Are you trying to butter me up?
    c) Isn't it a dog-eat-dog world?

ANSWERS TO LESSON 20, p. 193

Вставьте пропущенные слова:

1) After he was fired, Roger was going to send a nasty e-mail to his boss. But then he changed his mind and decided not to ____ his bridges.

   a) break   b) burn   c) destroy

2) Courtney's department is very efficient. She really runs a tight ____.

   a) ship   b) boat   c) raft

3) After spending several weeks out of the office, Phil felt ____ the loop.

   a) part of   b) in   c) out of

4) Jeremy brought his boss Betsy flowers on Boss's Day. He's always trying to ____ her up.

   a) please   b) oil   c) butter

5) If you bought a house closer to your office, you could ____ a bundle on gas.

   a) spare   b) save   c) make

6) Ever since Sam was passed up for a promotion last fall, he's had a chip on his ____.

   a) arm   b) shoulder   c) elbow

7) We need to think of some creative ways to increase our sales. Let's get together and bat ____ some ideas.

   a) around   b) about   c) off

8) You didn't reply to my urgent e-mail because your computer wasn't working? Spare me the ____ story!

   a) tragic   b) sad   c) sob

9) According to the rumor ____, Wayne has been having an affair with his administrative assistant for the past twenty years.

   a) mill   b) bin   c) machine

10) Zachary showed up late for work again, and then claimed he had a dentist appointment. He's up to his ____ tricks.

    a) new   b) old   c) favorite

11) I know you're not enjoying your international assignment, but you'll be leaving in a few months. For now, you'll just have to ____ and bear it.

    a) grin   b) smile   c) laugh

12) Shane is in charge of sales at our company, and our sales are down by 50 percent versus last year. His days are ____.

    a) limited   b) lettered   c) numbered

13) If you want to get ____ at this company, you're going to have to kiss up to your boss and put in long hours like everybody else.

    a) up   b) forward   c) ahead

14) You can try to talk me into going to the conference until you're ____ in the face. I've already decided I'm not going.

    a) green   b) blue   c) red

15) When Peter was told he would have to move into a much smaller office, he got really ____ out of shape.

    a) twisted   b) bent   c) stretched

ANSWERS TO REVIEW, p. 194

I don't know whether I'm coming or going.

Lesson 21

EXPLAINING THAT YOU'RE FEELING OVERWORKED

Mary is feeling overwhelmed between commitments at home and at work. Dan advises her to be patient and stay focused. Things will improve once their busy period at the office is over.

Мэри разрывается между домом и работой. Дэн советует ей запастись терпением и сконцентрироваться. Все образуется, как только в офисе пройдет авральный период.

Dan: Mary, why weren't you at the staff meeting this morning? We all missed you.

Mary: Oh, it completely **slipped my mind**.

Dan: How could you forget? These meetings are not *optional*.

Mary: I'm feeling so **stressed out** these days. Sometimes **I don't know whether I'm coming or going**!

Dan: Well, it *is* **crunch time** right now. Things will **settle down** after tax season is over.

Mary: I hope so. I am **wiped out** after putting in 60-hour weeks at the office and taking care of my five kids and sick mother.

Dan: Wow, you really do **have a lot on your plate**.

Mary: Yeah, I can hardly **keep my head above water**. Maybe I should **scale back my hours**.

Dan: Just **hang in there** a little longer. After April 15th, it'll quiet down around here. For now, **keep your nose to the grindstone** and focus on getting your most important work done.

Mary: You're right. I need to remember the **80/20 rule**. I get 80 percent of my results from just 20 percent of my activities. Now if I could only figure out what that 20 percent is!

IDIOMS & EXPRESSIONS – LESSON 21

(to) slip one's mind – to be forgotten or overlooked
забыть о чем-либо; упустить что-либо из виду; не обратить внимания; «выпало из головы», «отшибло память»

➤ Sorry I didn't send out that memo last Friday. To be honest with you, it **slipped my mind**.

Примечание. Обратите внимание на то, что подлежащее здесь "it", что делает эту фразу безличным оборотом, в отличие от "I forgot" – активного залога. Вы как бы снимаете с себя ответственность, говоря: "It slipped my mind".

---

stressed out – under severe strain; very anxious; very nervous
в стрессовом состоянии; очень нервный, озабоченный, утомленный

➤ After hearing a rumor that there were going to be layoffs at her company, Barbara was really **stressed out**.

I don't know whether I'm coming or going – I'm so busy, I can barely think clearly; I'm not focused; I'm distracted
совсем закрутиться, зашиться, запутаться в делах; я так занят, что едва ли в состоянии ясно мыслить; я не могу сосредоточиться

➤ I accidentally sent an e-mail complaining about my boss to the boss himself! **I don't whether I'm coming or going** today.

---

crunch time – a short period when there's high pressure to achieve a result
добиться необходимых результатов в сжатые сроки; кризисная ситуация; решающий для достижения цели момент

➤ It's **crunch time** for stem cell researchers in Korea. New government regulations may soon make their work illegal.

(to) settle down – to calm down; to become quiet
успокоиться; стабилизироваться; угомониться

➤ The mall is very busy in November and December, but after the holidays, things **settle down**.

---

wiped out – very tired; exhausted
уставший, измученный, измотанный; без сил; как выжатый лимон

➤ Ken traveled to Russia, India, and China all in one week. No wonder he's **wiped out**!

(to) have a lot on one's plate – to have a lot to do; to have too much to do; to have too much to cope with
иметь чересчур много дел; иметь слишком обширную программу

➤ Carlos turned down the project, explaining that he already **had a lot on his plate**.

Примечание. Встречается также вариант — to have too much on one's plate.

(to) keep one's head above water – to survive; to get by; to survive financial difficulties
держаться на плаву; не пойти ко дну; выжить; пережить финансовые трудности

➤ Thanks to this new contract, we'll be able to **keep our head above water** for another six months.

(to) scale back one's hours – to reduce the number of hours one works
сократить число рабочих часов

➤ When Christine had a baby, she decided to **scale back her hours** and just work part-time.

---

hang in there – be patient; don't get discouraged
потерпите еще немного; держитесь, не теряйте надежды

➤ Your company lost a million dollars last quarter? **Hang in there**. You'll do better next quarter.

(to) keep one's nose to the grindstone – to focus on one's work; to focus on working hard

сконцентрироваться на работе; побуждать кого-либо или самому работать без отдыха

➤ Unfortunately, I can't come to happy hour tonight. I need to **keep my nose to the grindstone** and finish a proposal I'm working on.

Происхождение. "Grindstone" – это точильный камень. Работая над точильным камнем, приходится нагибаться очень низко, почти касаться носом камня.

(the) 80/20 rule – the principle that 80 percent of results are achieved through just 20 percent of activities

правило 80/20 заключается в следующем: 80% результатов в бизнесе достигаются за 20% времени или усилий (или: 20% товара дают 80% прибыли; или: 20% преступников виновны в 80% преступлений, и т. д.)

➤ By applying the **80/20 rule**, Marcy was able to reduce the number of tasks she does during the work day.

✎ Practice the Idioms

Найдите наилучшую замену выделенным выражениям:

1) Kate said she didn't have time to help you? I'm not surprised, since **she has a lot on her plate right now**.
   a) she's very busy these days
   b) she's taken too much food
   c) she doesn't really like to help people

2) Instead of retiring, Joyce decided to keep working and just **scale back her hours**.
   a) increase the number of hours she works
   b) retire in a few years
   c) reduce the number of hours she works

130

3) You've been at the office every night until midnight for the past three months? **Hang in there.** In just a few more weeks, the busy period will probably be over.
    a) Quit your job.
    b) Be patient.
    c) Keep complaining.

4) Tanya works all day and goes to school every evening. No wonder she's **wiped out**.
    a) exhausted
    b) sick
    c) full of energy

5) At the tax consulting firm, March and April are **crunch time**.
    a) a relaxing time
    b) a slow period
    c) a very busy period

6) You asked me to buy you a bamboo vase on my business trip to Hanoi? I'm sorry, but **it slipped my mind!**
    a) you never asked me for that
    b) I forgot
    c) I didn't get a chance

7) Eva is working full-time while studying for her MBA and taking care of her two small kids. **I don't know how she can keep her head above water.**
    a) No wonder she has no time to go swimming.
    b) I don't know how she manages.
    c) I don't know what she does with all her free time.

8) If you want to pass the CPA exam, you'd better **keep your nose to the grindstone** and stop going out every night to party.
    a) focus on studying
    b) focus on having fun
    c) keep your nose out of other people's business

ANSWERS TO LESSON 21, p. 194

My stomach is killing me.

CALLING IN SICK

Maria calls her boss, Scott, to tell him she's not feeling well, and she's going to have to take a sick day. Fortunately, Scott is an understanding boss.

Мария звонит своему боссу Скотту, чтобы сообщить, что она нездорова и вынуждена взять больничный. К счастью, Скотт — начальник, который относится к людям с пониманием.

Maria: Hi, Scott, it's Maria.

Scott: Hey Maria. **What's up?**

Maria: I'm not feeling well today.

Scott: Oh yeah? What's wrong?

Maria: **My stomach is killing me.** Maybe it's the sushi I ate last night. I'm **as sick as a dog.**

Scott: Sara **called in sick** today also. And Kurt just told me he was feeling **under the weather** today. I'm **not feeling so hot** myself. Maybe **there's something going around.**

Maria: Well, I hope you don't catch it too.

Scott: I **can't afford to** get sick. I'm **up to my ears** in work.

Maria: I should be back in the office tomorrow.

Scott: Don't worry about that. You should stay home until you feel better.

Maria: I'll try to work from home this afternoon if I feel better.

Scott: **Take it easy** today. We want you back **in tip-top shape.**

IDIOMS & EXPRESSIONS – LESSON 22

What's up?

1) What's happening? What's new?
Как дела? Что случилось? Что нового?

➤ **What's up?** I haven't seen you in a long time.

2) A polite way of asking "What do you want?" when somebody calls or comes into your office.
Вежливый эквивалент прямого вопроса "What do you want?" (Что надо? Зачем пришел?), когда кто-то звонит или приходит к вам в офис.

➤ **"What's up?"** — "I came by to see if you're free for lunch today."

---

my stomach (*my head, my arm, etc...*) is killing me – my stomach (my head, my arm, etc...) hurts very badly
у меня страшно болит живот (голова, рука и т. д.); я мучаюсь (страдаю) от чего-либо

➤ Liz left the office early today. **Her head was killing her.**

---

as sick as a dog – very sick
чувствовать себя очень плохо, скверно (часто в значении: испытывать приступы тошноты, рвоты)

➤ Joe got the flu and was **as sick as a dog** for a week.

(to) call in sick – to phone into the office and say you're sick
звонить в офис, сообщая о своей болезни; брать больничный

➤ Try not to **call in sick** too often. Employers don't like it.

---

under the weather – not feeling well
плохо себя чувствовать; недомогать; хандрить

➤ "You look pale. Is everything okay?" — "Not really. I'm feeling **under the weather**."

(to) not feel so hot – to feel sick; to not feel well
чувствовать себя не лучшим образом

➤ Jacob canceled our meeting for this afternoon. He said he **wasn't feeling so hot.**

there's something going around – there's an illness traveling around the office; many people are getting sick from some illness

вокруг происходит что-то неладное; в офисе гуляет эпидемия; часты случаи заболевания сотрудников

➤ Be sure to wash your hands often. **There's something going around the office**, and you don't want to catch it.

---

can't afford to – don't have time for; don't want to

не могу себе позволить что-либо (нет времени, не по карману и т. д.)

➤ Sorry, I **can't afford to** sit here and argue with you. I've got a lot of work to do.

---

up to one's ears in work – to have a lot of work; to have too much work

быть по уши загруженным работой; быть с головой в работе; иметь непочатый край работы

➤ Bill is **up to his ears in work**. He won't be able to meet with you until next week.

(to) take it easy – to relax; to rest; to not do too much

расслабиться; не волноваться; не принимать близко к сердцу; проще смотреть на вещи; не усердствовать

➤ You worry too much about everything. You need to just **take it easy**.

---

in tip-top shape – in great condition; completely healthy

в прекрасном состоянии; в хорошей форме; в лучшем виде

➤ Be sure you're **in tip-top shape** next week for our trip to Beijing.

✎ PRACTICE THE IDIOMS

Заполните пропуски, используя следующие идиомы:

killing me	**take it easy**
in tip-top shape	**under the weather**
up to my ears in work	**call in sick**
I'm not feeling so hot	**there's something going around**

Diana woke up this morning feeling _____(1)_____. "What's wrong?" her husband Boris asked. "My head is _____(2)_____," she replied. Boris handed her the phone and suggested that she _____(3)_____. "But I can't stay home today. I've got too much to do at the office," she said. "I'm _____(4)_____." Boris told her that the work could wait.

Diana took the phone and called her boss. "_____(5)_____," said Diana. Her boss replied, "It looks like _____(6)_____ the office. Several other people have also called in sick today. Just _____(7)_____ today and hopefully tomorrow you'll be _____(8)_____." Diana was grateful that she had such an understanding boss. She rolled over and went back to sleep.

ANSWERS TO LESSON 22, p. 194

REQUESTING A BANK LOAN

Ivan meets with Gina, a loan officer at L&S Bank, about getting a loan to start a new coffee shop. When Gina reviews his financial forecasts and suggests some changes, Ivan is angry at first but then decides to go along with it.

Иван встречается с Джиной, специалистом банка L&S по предоставлению кредитов, с тем, чтобы получить ссуду на открытие нового кафе. Когда Джина, ознакомившись с его финансовыми прогнозами, предлагает некоторые изменения, Иван сначала сердится, но потом решает с этим согласиться.

Ivan: I'm here to see about getting a $100,000 loan to start a Coffee Shack *franchise*.

Gina: I see from your application that you've already got two franchise businesses **under your belt** — both Subway sandwich shops. That's certainly **nothing to sneeze at**.

Ivan: Thank you. Now that I **know the franchise business inside and out**, I'd like to expand.

Gina: Well, Subway is a sandwich shop. Now you're talking about a coffee house. That's an entirely **different animal**.

Ivan: Sure, there may be a thing or two to learn, but it should be more or less a **no-brainer**.

Gina: I see from your business plan that you're basing all of your profit estimates on the profits you made from one of your Subway shops. I don't think that's right. You're **comparing apples to oranges**.

Ivan: Apples? Oranges? I didn't know we were talking about fruit now. Maybe I should open up a *fruit smoothie* shop instead!

137

Gina: Ha ha. Well, at least you haven't lost your sense of humor!

Ivan: Well, seriously, what do you want me to do?

Gina: Go **back to the drawing board**. Make some new calculations based on selling coffee, not sandwiches. Then the loan will be **in the bag**.

Ivan: If you're going to make me **jump through hoops** to get this loan, I'll just have to take my business to a different bank.

Gina: You're **missing the point** here. I'm not trying to make your life difficult. I'm just suggesting you **beef up** your business plan so my boss will approve your loan.

Ivan: Well, in that case, maybe I will go **back to the drawing board**.

IDIOMS & EXPRESSIONS – LESSON 23

(to have or to get) under one's belt – to have or to get experience
иметь или приобрести опыт в чем-либо; иметь за плечами опыт работы; набить руку на чем-либо

➤ Before you start your own coffee shop, you should work at Starbucks to **get some experience under your belt**.

---

nothing to sneeze at – not insignificant; impressive
не пустяк; не шутка; не фунт изюму; с этим надо считаться!

➤ This year, our company opened 15 new sales offices overseas. That's **nothing to sneeze at**!

(to) know something inside and out – to know something very well
знать что-либо досконально; изучить вдоль и поперек; быть хорошо осведомленным; разбираться в тонкостях

➤ If you're having a problem with your presentation, ask Pam for help. She **knows PowerPoint inside and out**.

SYNONYM: to know like the back of one's hand. Example: Pam **knows PowerPoint like the back of her hand**.

different animal – something entirely different
что-либо совершенно отличное, иное, непохожее

➤ The Gap had many years of experience selling clothing through retail stores. When they started the Gap.com, they found out that selling online was a **different animal**.

no-brainer – an easy decision; an obvious choice
простое, не требующее большого ума решение; что-либо очевидное

➤ Most of our clients are based in Korea, so it's a **no-brainer** to open an office there.

(to) compare apples to oranges – to compare two unlike things; to make an invalid comparison
сравнивать несравнимые вещи; досл.: сравнивать яблоки с апельсинами

➤ Comparing a night at EconoLodge with a night at the Four Seasons is like **comparing apples to oranges**. One is a budget motel, and the other is a luxury hotel.

Примечание. Вы можете также встретить выражение "compare apples to apples", которое означает «сравнивать две однотипные вещи» и которое, в отличие от сопоставления яблок с апельсинами, вполне допустимо.

(to) go back to the drawing board – to start a task over because the last try failed; to start again from the beginning
начать с чистого листа; начать все сначала в связи с неудачной последней попыткой

➤ We didn't like the print advertisement our ad agency designed, so we asked them to **go back to the drawing board**.

in the bag – a sure thing
дело в шляпе; верное дело; решенный вопрос

➤ Boeing executives thought that the new military contract was **in the bag** and were surprised when it was awarded to Airbus instead.

SYNONYM: a done deal. Example: Boeing executives thought the new military contract was **a done deal**.

(to) jump through hoops – to go through a lot of difficult work for something; to face many bureaucratic obstacles
преодолевать препятствия ради чего-либо; сталкиваться с бюрократическими препонами; досл.: прыгать через обручи

> We had to **jump through hoops** to get our visas to Russia, but we finally got them.

(to) miss the point – to not understand
упустить суть; не понять главного

> You're **missing the point**. Your son wants an expensive new cell phone so he can impress his friends, not because he actually needs all of those bells and whistles.

---

beef up – *see Lesson 5*

✍ PRACTICE THE IDIOMS

Найдите наилучшую замену выделенным выражениям:

1) Procter & Gamble had to **jump through hoops** to get its new drug approved by the Food and Drug Administration.
   a) ask the right people
   b) take many steps
   c) show proven results

2) Nora had a very good job interview with the bank. She thinks **the job is in the bag.**
   a) she'll get an offer
   b) she'll get a rejection letter
   c) she'll get a bag with the bank's logo on it

3) Madeleine Albright made many connections while she was U.S. Secretary of State. It was **a no-brainer** for her to open a political consulting firm after she left office.
   a) a poor decision
   b) a logical decision
   c) a tough decision

4) When the popular coffee house announced it would start staying open until midnight and start serving beer, many loyal customers feared it would **become a different animal**.
   a) become a hangout for dogs and cats
   b) change in character
   c) become an even better coffee house

5) I know you were hoping for a higher bonus, but $5,000 is **nothing to sneeze at!**
   a) less than you deserve
   b) disappointing
   c) a good amount of money

6) Of course, I prefer Dom Perignon champagne over a $4 bottle of sparking wine, but **comparing the two is like comparing apples to oranges**.
   a) you can't really compare the two
   b) one is fruitier than the other
   c) it makes sense to compare the two

7) If you need advice on where to set up your new manufacturing facility in China, talk to Stan. **He knows China inside and out.**
   a) He's been to China a few times.
   b) He speaks Chinese.
   c) He knows China very well.

8) Chris spent a year working as an intern at Chelsea Brewing Company in order to **get some experience under his belt**. Then he opened his own microbrewery.
   a) have a good time
   b) make some money
   c) gain experience

ANSWERS TO LESSON 23, p. 194

You really need a full page ad to make a splash.

NEGOTIATING A PURCHASE

Jack, owner of Jack's Party Store, is negotiating to buy an advertisement in the Newport Times. Dave is an ad salesman with the newspaper.

Джек, владелец магазина Jack's Party, ведет переговоры о размещении рекламного объявления в газете Newport Times. Дэйв работает рекламным агентом в газете.

Jack: My store is having a big sale next week. I'd like to buy a small advertisement in the Sunday edition of the *Newport Times*. How much would a quarter page cost?

Dave: A quarter page ad costs $250. What you really need is a full page ad if you want to **make a splash**. That would be $900. I better reserve that for you before we run out of space.

Jack: Don't try to give me **the hard sell**. Nine hundred bucks would **break my budget**!

Dave: Okay, so we're looking at a quarter page. For another $200 I can make it a full color ad. Color would give you **more bang for the buck**.

Jack: Of course color is better than black and white. That's a **no-brainer**! Can you **throw that in at no extra charge**?

Dave: Sorry, **no can do**.

Jack: Your competitor, the *Newport Bulletin*, is offering me a quarter page color ad for $300. That's very attractive since I'm **on a tight budget**.

Dave: The *Newport Bulletin*? This is **off the record**, but you really don't want to advertise in that *rag!* Nobody reads it.

Jack: Here's my final offer: I'll take a quarter page color ad in your paper for $350 and not a penny more.

Dave: How about we find a **happy medium**. I'll give it to you for $400.

Jack: Please don't try to **nickel-and-dime** me. I'm **standing firm** at $350.

Dave: Okay, I don't want to spend all afternoon arguing. **It's a deal.**

IDIOMS & EXPRESSIONS – LESSON 24

(to) make a splash – to make a big impact; to get a lot of attention
произвести сенсацию, фурор; привлечь всеобщее внимание; наделать много шума; досл.: поднять брызги

➤ Careerbuilder.com **made a splash** with its funny TV commercials starring chimpanzees.

(the) hard sell – an aggressive way of selling
агрессивный, навязчивый, чересчур настойчивый способ прода-жи товара или услуг

➤ Car salesmen have a reputation for using **the hard sell** on their customers.

Примечание. Антоним "hard sell" – "soft sell", что означает «про-давать, не используя агрессивную тактику».

(to) break one's budget – to cost much more than one wants to pay; to cost more than one can afford
превысить бюджет; стоить больше, чем кто-либо хотел бы запла-тить; быть не по карману; бюджет трещит по швам

➤ The advertising expenses you proposed are too high. We don't want to **break our budget**.

more bang for the buck – more value for one's money; a higher return on investment
получить на малое вложение гораздо больше, чем предполагалось; больший возврат на единицу вложения

➤ We should add some more features to our products. Customers are starting to demand **more bang for the buck**.

Примечание. Слово "buck" означает «доллар» (сленг).

no-brainer – *see Lesson 23*

(to) throw in something – to include something (usually for free, as part of the sale)
добавить что-либо к продаваемому товару, обычно бесплатно, как часть сделки; а также в значении: мобилизовать, устремить, «бросить» (о внутреннем потенциале, возможностях и т. д.)

➤ Order our new exercise equipment today, and we'll **throw in** a free how-to video.

at no extra charge – for free; for no additional money
даром; бесплатно; без дополнительной оплаты

➤ If you buy a ticket to the museum, you can visit the special Van Gogh exhibit **at no extra charge**.

no can do – I can't do that; I'm unable to satisfy your request
я не могу это сделать; я не в состоянии удовлетворить вашу просьбу

➤ "We'd like you to work on Thanksgiving Day this year." — "Sorry, **no can do**. I've already got plans."

(to be) on a tight budget – to not have much money to spend; to have a limited amount to spend
быть на ограниченном бюджете; не иметь много денег на расходы; иметь лимитированную сумму на расходы

➤ Can you give us a better price on the printing job? We're **on a tight budget**.

off the record – just between us; unofficial; not to be repeated to others
между нами говоря; неофициально; не для посторонних; не для протокола

➤ This is **off the record**, but I wouldn't trust Todd to do the financial analysis. He's careless and often makes mistakes.

---

happy medium – a compromise
золотая середина; компромисс

➤ Lee wants to spend $100,000 re-designing our entire website, while Nicole suggests just adding a few new links. We need to find a **happy medium**.

(to) nickel-and-dime – to negotiate over very small sums; to try to get a better financial deal, in a negative way
торговаться из-за каждой копейки; мелочиться; стараться выторговать в свою пользу (обычно в негативном плане)

➤ We don't want to **nickel-and-dime** you, but we'd really appreciate it if you would lower your estimate by another $250.

Происхождение. Пенни, никель, дайм – самые мелкие монеты в США. Эти слова часто употребляются в американских идиомах, связанных с деньгами, финансами и т. д. Так например, "pretty penny" (см. главу 9), "dime a dozen" (дешевый, не имеющий особой ценности), "pinch pennies" (экономя на каждой копейке).

(to) stand firm – to remain at; to not offer more than; to resist; to refuse to yield to
твердо стоять на своем; гнуть свою линию; не идти на уступки

➤ Pemco Industries put a lot of pressure on Peggy to resign, but she **stood firm** and refused to leave her job voluntarily.

---

it's a deal – I agree (to a proposal or offer)
Согласен! По рукам! (принимая предложение)

➤ "If you let me leave at noon on Friday, I'll stay here late on Thursday." — "Okay, **it's a deal**."

✎ PRACTICE THE IDIOMS

Заполните пропуски, используя следующие идиомы:

the hard sell	it's a deal
no can do	at no extra charge
more bang for the buck	break my budget
nickel-and-dime	on a tight budget

Tina: Hi, I'm in the market for a new car, and I like the Mini Cooper. Would you recommend the base model or the Cooper S model?

Eric: The Cooper S. It gives you _____(1)_____. It's got a lot more power. I would also suggest you upgrade to leather seats.

Tina: How much extra are those?

Eric: $1300.

Tina: Forget it! That's too much. It would _____(2)_____.

Eric: Okay, I'm just making a suggestion. I'm not trying to give you _____(3)_____. However, you probably will want to get the heated front seats.

Tina: Can you throw those in _____(4)_____?

Eric: Sorry, _____(5)_____.

Tina: Well, how much would the car cost without all the bells and whistles?

Eric: $20,500.

Tina: I don't want to _____(6)_____ you, but I am a single mother with four kids and I'm _____(7)_____. Can you offer it to me for $18,500?

Eric: I'm afraid not. But I could go to $19,500.

Tina: Okay, _____(8)_____.

ANSWERS TO LESSON 24, p. 194

You've got a knack for sales.

CONDUCTING A PERFORMANCE REVIEW

It's annual performance review time. John meets with his boss to go over his performance for the past year, hear about his strengths and weaknesses, and find out about his salary increase.

Пришло время ежегодной профессиональной аттестации. Джон встречается с боссом для того, чтобы обсудить свои рабочие показатели за прошедший год, услышать о своих сильных и слабых сторонах, а также узнать о прибавке к зарплате.

Sara: During the first half of the year, your performance was **not so hot**. But then you **did a 180**, and you started doing great.

John: Really? I was that bad at the beginning of the year?

Sara: I think it was because you were new here, and it took you a while **to get up to speed**. The most important thing is that you're now a valuable member of the team.

John: That's nice to hear.

Sara: You've **got a knack for** sales. These past few months, I've also seen your communication skills improve. You're great at **keeping people in the loop** and making sure we all know what's going on with your accounts.

John: Thanks. I do **pride myself on** my communication skills.

Sara: Of course, you still have some **opportunity areas** that I'd like you to work on, starting with your *analytical* skills. Sometimes I can't **make heads or tails of** your sales forecasts.

John: How would you suggest I work on that?

Sara: I'm going to send you to a training class. Then we'll **take it from there**.

149

John: Great. I love attending classes!

Sara: We'll be raising your salary by 5 percent to $60,000. And, if you really go **beyond the call of duty**, you'll also receive a bonus at the end of the year.

IDIOMS & EXPRESSIONS – LESSON 25

not so hot – not very good
не слишком хорошо; не блестяще; так себе; могло быть лучше

➤ This new advertising campaign is **not so hot**. I think we can do better next time.

(to) do a 180 – to turn around; to improve a lot
развернуться на 180 градусов; кардинально изменить свою позицию; изменить что-либо к лучшему

➤ The company used to make all its products in the USA, but then they **did a 180**. Now all of their products are made in China.

Примечание. Эта фраза подразумевает 180 градусов (половина от окружности в 360 градусов). Поворот на 180 градусов означает, что вы поменяли направление движения на противоположное.

(to) get up to speed – to learn how to do a new job or a new task
набрать скорость, обороты; научиться выполнять новую работу или проект; войти в ритм новой работы

➤ Nick had to start making sales calls his first week on the job, so he didn't have much time to **get up to speed**.

(to) have a knack for something – to be skilled at something; to be naturally good at something (either in a positive or a negative way)
отличаться умением, сноровкой; быть ловким в чем-либо (как в хорошем, так и в плохом смысле)

➤ I can't believe Joe told you that your tie looks old-fashioned. He has **a knack for** making people feel bad.

(to) keep someone in the loop – to let someone know what's going on; to provide regular updates
держать кого-либо в курсе дела; регулярно информировать

➤ The finance manager doesn't need to be invited to every meeting, but be sure to **keep her in the loop**.

(to) pride oneself on something – to be proud of; to recognize one's own skill in a certain area
гордиться чем-либо; осознавать свое умение в какой-либо сфере

➤ Naomi **prides herself on** her excellent people skills.

---

opportunity areas – weaknesses; skills that need to be improved
нереализованные возможности; слабые стороны; навыки, требующие усовершенствования

➤ The human resource manager spent 45 minutes with Kristen, reviewing her **opportunity areas**.

(to) not be able to make heads or tails of – to be unable to interpret
быть не в состоянии что-либо понять, разобраться что к чему

➤ Magna Corporation's new employee health plan is very confusing. The employees **can't make heads or tails of it**.

(to) take it from there – to wait and see what else needs to be done; to take just one step and then decide what to do next
сделать первый шаг и осмотреться, выждать, чтобы определить, что делать дальше; двигаться постепенно

➤ Let's start by calculating how much it would cost to open an office in Budapest, and then we'll **take it from there**.

---

beyond the call of duty – more than is expected or required
превзойти все ожидания (в работе); сделать больше, чем ожидалось или требовалось

➤ Susan worked all day Sunday baking chocolate chip cookies for the office. That was **beyond the call of duty**.

Примечание. Встречается также вариант — above and beyond the call of duty.

🖎 PRACTICE THE IDIOMS

Найдите наилучшую замену выделенным выражениям:

1) Susan said she'd be happy to bring chocolate chip cookies to the office. **She prides herself on being a good baker.**
   a) She mistakenly thinks she can bake.
   b) She's proud of her skills as a baker.
   c) She bakes chocolate chip cookies every day.

2) Neil's attitude was bad last year, but this year he's **done a 180**.
   a) developed an even worse attitude
   b) dramatically improved his attitude
   c) left the job

3) The new government regulations are very complicated. **We can't make heads or tails of them.**
   a) We think they're excellent.
   b) We think they're very bad.
   c) We can't understand them at all.

4) Although you've improved your written communication skills over the past year, this is still an **opportunity area for you**.
   a) an area where you need to improve further
   b) an area where you've already made enough progress
   c) an area where you'll find exciting opportunities

5) If you need help with your new logo, ask Molly. **She's got a knack for graphic design.**
   a) She used to be a graphic designer.
   b) She knows several good graphic designers.
   c) She's very good at graphic design.

6) You spent 14 hours proofreading my report? **That was beyond the call of duty.**
   a) That was more than I expected.
   b) You shouldn't have bothered.
   c) You were just doing your job.

7) Please **keep me in the loop regarding** your vacation plans. I need to know when you're not going to be in the office.
   a) keep me updated about
   b) don't bother telling me about
   c) let everybody in the office know about

8) Vladimir's new job at the lab is very complicated. It may take him a few months to **get up to speed**.
   a) feel like he's got too much work to do
   b) feel comfortable doing the job
   c) feel like the job is too difficult for him

ANSWERS TO LESSON 25, p. 194

REVIEW FOR LESSONS 21-25

Вставьте пропущенные слова:

1) Companies shouldn't make investors _____ through hoops to get financial information.

    a) hop   b) skip   c) jump

2) After hosting 25 visitors from Japan for four weeks, Marcy was wiped _____.

    a) in   b) out   c) up

3) Jerry suggested that I buy the Dell Pocket DJ instead of the Apple iPod Mini. He said I'd get more bang for the ____.

    a) dollar   b) buck   c) cash

4) The loan officer at the bank said our business plan was very confusing. He couldn't make heads or ____ of it.

    a) tails   b) necks   c) sense

5) I'm sorry I won't be able to come to your presentation. I'm up to my ____ in work.

    a) eyes   b) ears   c) head

6) Sorry I forgot to book your airplane tickets. It ____ my mind.

    a) slipped   b) escaped   c) skipped

7) Oil prices have come down recently, but $55 a barrel is still nothing to ____ at.

    a) laugh   b) sniff   c) sneeze

8) That e-mail you sent me with the details about your project was very helpful. Thanks for keeping me ____ the loop.

   a) within   b) in   c) with

9) Between working full-time at the bank and volunteering as a fireman on weekends, Neil has a lot on his ____.

   a) table   b) plate   c) desk

10) Wal-Mart set up a huge display of under $20 Christmas gifts. It's great for people on a ____ budget.

   a) big   b) loose   c) tight

11) No wonder Ken is so rich. He has a knack ____ picking winning stocks!

   a) for   b) with   c) in

12) When Wendy and Jim bought the leather couch for $1600, the furniture store agreed to throw ____ a $200 chair at no extra charge.

   a) up   b) out   c) in

13) Andy won't be in today. He's feeling ____ the weather.

   a) over   b) under   c) beyond

14) Things have been very busy at the office lately. I hope they'll settle ____ soon.

   a) down   b) over   c) up

15) We want to move our company headquarters to a city. Chicago is too large, but Salt Lake City is too small. Atlanta might be a ____ medium.

   a) perfect   b) happy   c) mixed

ANSWERS TO REVIEW, p. 195

Lesson 26

PROMOTING AN EMPLOYEE

Steve is meeting with his boss, Kurt, to review his performance. Kurt promotes Steve to the position of marketing director.

Стив встречается со своим начальником Куртом, чтобы обсудить свои служебные успехи. Курт выдвигает Стива на должность директора по маркетингу.

Kurt: Steve, your performance over the past year has been excellent. You've only been here a year, but you **hit the ground running**.

Steve: Thank you. It's nice to be appreciated!

Kurt: You're **an "A" player** here — a real star. You've really **earned your keep**. You're great at motivating your employees, and you're always willing to **go the extra mile**.

Steve: Thanks, Kurt. I really enjoy my work here.

Kurt: I'm going to **take you into my confidence**. Steve, this past year has been really challenging. Everybody hasn't **made the grade**.

Steve: Right. I just heard that Dan is going to be **given his walking papers.**

Kurt: Yes, he'll be **leaving us**. I'll be **breaking the news** to him this afternoon. But the good news is that I'm promoting you to marketing director.

Steve: Wow, that is good news. Thank you!

Kurt: No need to thank me. You're a real **go-getter** and you earned it. The new position comes with a 10 percent raise and several *perks*, including an extra week of vacation.

Steve: Will I get a company car too?

Kurt: Don't **push your luck.** But if you **play your cards right**, maybe in a few years. Ten years **down the road**, I can even see you in a *corner office*.

Steve: Thanks, Kurt.

Kurt: No, Steve, thank you. **Keep up the good work!**

IDIOMS & EXPRESSIONS – LESSON 26

(to) hit the ground running – to have a successful start to a new job; to start at full speed
успешно приступить к новой работе; с ходу взяться за дело.

➤ We need to hire somebody who can **hit the ground running**. We don't have time to train anybody.

(an) "A" player – a top performer; a superior employee
отличный работник; один из лучших служащих

➤ We need to ensure that our **"A" players** don't leave our company and take jobs with the competition.

Примечание. Некоторые корпорации оценивают своих сотрудников в соответствии с начальными буквами алфавита, как это принято в школьной системе США: A, B и C. В высшую категорию попадают примерно 10%-20% – это "A" players; затем следуют "B" players, составляющие примерно 70%-80%; и, наконец, "C" players, которые представляют оставшиеся 10% и, как правило, в компании надолго не задерживаются.

(to) earn one's keep – to deserve what one is paid; to deserve to be in the position one is in; to contribute one's share
отрабатывать свою зарплату; не даром есть свой хлеб

➤ Carl stands around flirting with the receptionist all day instead of working. He's not **earning his keep**.

(to) go the extra mile – to do more than what is expected or required
делать больше, чем ожидается или требуется; делать все возможное и сверх того; приложить все силы

➤ The graphic designer showed us 25 possible designs for the cover of our new newsletter. He really **went the extra mile**.

(to) take someone into one's confidence – to tell somebody something confidentially; to tell somebody sensitive information
довериться кому-либо; делиться конфиденциальной информацией

➤ Linda **took Dan into her confidence** and told him that several people in the department were going to get laid off.

(to) make the grade – to succeed; to fulfill the requirements
достичь цели; выполнить обязательства; преуспеть

➤ After it was clear that Nathan **made the grade** as an account executive at the ad agency, he was promoted to account director.

---

leaving us – leaving the company (often a polite way of saying somebody's been fired)
Х уходит из компании, покидает нас (часто это вежливый, способ сообщить о том, что кого-то увольняют)

➤ We're sad to say that after ten years here, Jill will be **leaving us** to pursue more time with her family.

(to) break the news – to make something known (often something unpleasant)
объявить, сообщить о чем-либо (часто о чем-то неприятном)

➤ Sorry to **break the news**, but your competitors have come out with a product that works much better than yours and costs half the price.

---

go-getter – a hard-working, ambitious person; someone very good at delivering results at work
прилежный, трудолюбивый, целеустремленный человек; предприимчивый, результативный работник

➤ Carol is a real **go-getter**, so nobody was surprised when she was promoted to vice president of the bank.

don't push your luck – don't try to get too much; be satisfied with what you've already gotten and don't try to get more
не искушайте судьбу; не спугните фортуну; довольствуйтесь тем что есть и не пытайтесь заполучить что-то большее

➤ If your boss has already agreed to send you to two training courses this year, **don't push your luck** and ask for a third.

Примечание. Встречается также вариант "don't press your luck".

(to) play one's cards right – to make the most of one's opportunities or situation
максимально выгодно использовать случай или ситуацию; верно разыграть карту

➤ Louis **played his cards right** at the law firm, and he was made partner after only five years there.

down the road – in the future
в перспективе; в будущем; в конечном счете

➤ Jay doesn't want to work for a big company forever. Five years **down the road**, he'd like to start his own business.

Keep up the good work! – continue as you are; you're doing well, continue to do well
продолжайте в том же духе; не сбавляйте темпа

➤ Team, we just had our best year in company history. **Keep up the good work!**

✎ PRACTICE THE IDIOMS

Найдите наилучшую замену выделенным выражениям:

1) Paula is **a real go-getter**. No wonder she was our top salesperson last month!
   a) very good at making friends
   b) a reliable, kind person
   c) very effective at her job

2) My company just agreed to give me a company car, so I'm not going to **push my luck** by asking for a large raise now.
   a) see if I can get more good luck
   b) see what more I can get
   c) make my boss happy

3) When Keith didn't **make the grade** as a professional athlete, he decided to become a high school football coach instead.
   a) succeed
   b) fail
   c) get good grades

4) Kate is interested in working internationally, and she hopes to get a job in Europe **down the road**.
   a) after she retires
   b) close to home
   c) in the future

5) Sure, Michelle earns more money than any of us and has the biggest office, but **she's earned her keep**.
   a) she earns a lot of money
   b) she just got lucky
   c) she deserves it

6) **I'm not sure how to break the news**, but our company is bankrupt and our offices will close down next week.
   a) I've got some wonderful news to tell you
   b) This is difficult to discuss
   c) I'm not sure whether or not this is true

7) Nordstrom's department stores are famous for their customer service. They're always willing to **go the extra mile** to please their customers.
   a) travel long distances
   b) do a lot
   c) do nothing

8) Sheryl didn't get the job at *Newsweek*. They told her they needed somebody with more experience **who could hit the ground running**.
   a) who would run away from the job after a short period
   b) who could tell everybody else how to do their jobs
   c) who would learn quickly how to do the job

ANSWERS TO LESSON 26, p. 195

You didn't lift a finger on that project.

FIRING SOMEBODY

Kurt has the difficult task of firing Dan. Dan's been with the company since the beginning and is a friend of Kurt's. Dan is surprised and upset with the news.

Перед Куртом стоит трудная задача – уволить Дэна. Дэн работает в компании с самого ее основания, и к тому же он – друг Курта. Дэн очень удивлен и расстроен этим известием.

Kurt: Dan, **your work has slipped**. You've been here for 15 years, and I think you're just **burned out**.

Dan: What are you talking about? I'm **at the top of my game**. I just managed our biggest project in years.

Kurt: You can't **take credit for** that. You **didn't lift a finger** on that project. You were on vacation in Hawaii for three weeks while Steve and Sally were doing all the work.

Dan: I'm not good at **reading between the lines**. Please just **cut to the chase**. What are you trying to say?

Kurt: Dan, Swift Shoes is *downsizing*. This is really difficult, but we're going to have to **let you go**.

Dan: What? I helped **build this company from the ground up**! You can't fire me now.

Kurt: I don't want to, but **my hands are tied**. Our president has told me to **reduce headcount** by 50 percent.

Dan: I thought you and I were friends, but **when push comes to shove**, I guess our friendship isn't worth anything.

Kurt: Of course we're still friends, but business is business.

Dan: I don't agree with that. I would never fire a friend…after all those times Kathleen and I invited you and Donna to dinner at our home!

Kurt: Dan, I want you to leave Swift Shoes on friendly terms. **No hard feelings**. To **soften the blow**, we're going to give you a generous *severance package*.

IDIOMS & EXPRESSIONS – LESSON 27

one's work has slipped – one's performance has gotten worse; one is not doing one's job properly
чьи-либо рабочие показатели ухудшились; кто-либо не выполняет свою работу как положено

> What's going on with Larry? He used to be very good at his job, but recently **his work has slipped**.

(to be) burned out – to be extremely tired; to lose effectiveness because of doing a job for too long
быть измученным работой; исчерпать себя; понизить произ-водительность (часто выполняя одну и ту же работу слишком долго)

> After working 80-hour weeks at the investment bank for many years, Jim was **burned out**.

(to be) at the top of one's game – to be performing at the top of one's abilities; to be performing very well
работать на пике своих способностей, с максимальной отдачей; блестяще исполнять рабочие обязанности

> Last year, Nick brought in over $5 million in new business to the agency. He's **at the top of his game**.

(to) take credit for something – to claim recognition for something
ставить себе в заслугу что-либо; претендовать на похвалу или одобрение за хорошую работу

> Joan came up with the idea of selling the company's products at Costco, but her boss **took the credit for it**.

(to) not lift a finger – to not help at all; to do nothing
пальцем не пошевелить; палец о палец не ударить

➤ While everybody else was working hard to finish the project, Todd was chatting with his friend and **didn't lift a finger**.

(to) read between the lines – to understand unclear or indirect communication; to interpret something from hints or suggestions
читать между строк; понимать с полуслова; схватывать на лету

➤ Your boss told you to take a very long vacation? **Read between the lines**: he's suggesting you leave the company!

Происхождение. Это выражение связано с практикой ведения секретной переписки с использованием невидимых чернил. При особой обработке, например, с помощью лимонного сока, секретное послание проступало между строк обычного письма. Отсюда пошло «читать между строк» в значении «понимать скрытый смысл».

(to) cut to the chase – to get to the point; to tell the most important part of the story
перейти к сути (разговора, события), к развязке, к кульминации

➤ I don't have time to listen to a long explanation of why you didn't finish this project on time. Please **cut to the chase**.

Происхождение. В фильмах приключенческого жанра "chase" относится к самому интересному моменту, развязке, когда драма достигает кульминации. Некоторые предпочитают посмотреть только этот отрывок или эпизод из всего фильма. Начать с развязки, чтобы сразу понять суть.

(to) let someone go – to fire someone
уволить кого-либо; дать уйти

➤ Mepstein Industries **let their accountant go** after he made a major mistake calculating the company's tax bill.

(to) build something from the ground up – to develop a company, a business, or a department from its beginnings; to build a successful operation from scratch
стоять у истоков компании; закладывать фундамент компании или бизнеса; построить успешный бизнес с нуля

➤ Autumn Moon Vineyards doesn't yet have a marketing department. They're going to have to **build one from the ground up**.

my hands are tied – there's nothing I can do; I'm stuck; I have no alternatives
у меня связаны руки; ничем не могу помочь; у меня нет выбора

➤ I would like to give you a discount on this project, but my boss will not allow it. I'm sorry, but **my hands are tied**.

(to) reduce headcount – to lay off or fire workers
сократить штат сотрудников; уволить часть персонала

➤ When Lucent's business was in trouble, they announced they would **reduce headcount** by at least 10,000 employees.

Примечание. "Headcount" – это штат, общее число сотрудников, работающих в какой-либо организации. Во многих компаниях, когда заходит речь о массовых увольнениях или сокращениях, избегают говорить "laying people off" («увольнение людей»), полагая, что это выражение звучит холодно и негуманно по отношению к людям. Считается, что выражение "reduce headcount" («сокращение штата», «сокращение общей численности») имеет более наукообразное и отвлеченное звучание и воспринимается не так персонально.

SYNONYM: to downsize

---

when push comes to shove – when really tested; when it really counts; when there's no more time left to hesitate or think about what action to take
в решающий момент; когда доходит до дела; когда идет настоящая проверка и подсчет; когда нет времени на раздумья, так как необходимо перейти к действиям

➤ Many people say they are worried about the environment, but **when push comes to shove**, how many people are willing to pay extra for environmentally-friendly products?

SYNONYM: when you come right down to it

---

no hard feelings – no anger; no bitterness
не держать зла на кого-либо; не носить камень за пазухой

➤ Even though Hewlett-Packard didn't give Justin a job offer, he has **no hard feelings** towards them.

✑ PRACTICE THE IDIOMS

Заполните пропуски, используя следующие идиомы:

no hard feelings	work has really slipped
let them go	build the company from the ground up
her hands are tied	burned out
take credit for	at the top of her game
reduce headcount	lifted a finger

Liz is in a difficult position. Her boss has told her to _____(1)_____ since the company is in financial trouble. Liz only has three employees: Brian, Rachel, and Pam. Brian and Rachel are doing great work, so she can't afford to _____(2)_____. Pam isn't doing so well. In fact, over the past year her _____(3)_____. On a recent project, Brian and Rachel did 90 percent of the work and Pam barely _____(4)_____. Later, Pam declared the project a "great success" and tried to _____(5)_____ it.

It's true that Pam helped _____(6)_____ and has been a loyal employee over the past decade. Unfortunately, she's no longer _____(7)_____. Liz thinks Pam worked too hard in the past and is now _____(8)_____. Liz likes Pam, and would prefer not to fire her. But _____(9)_____. Liz hopes there will be _____(10)_____ after she tells Pam the bad news.

ANSWERS TO LESSON 27, p. 195

In my last job, I wore many hats.

JOB INTERVIEW 1

Donna, a Human Resources Manager, is interviewing Marina for a sales position.

Донна, менеджер по трудовым ресурсам, интервьюирует Марину на должность специалиста по продажам.

Donna: Tell me about your most recent work experience.

Marina: Right now I'm **between jobs**. In my last position, I was a marketing associate at Comtek International. I was there for two and a half years.

Donna: I know I've heard of them, but I'm **drawing a blank** right now. What do they do?

Marina: They produced international trade fairs. They were **bought out** last month by a much larger company and all of us were **let go**.

Donna: I see from your résumé that you also worked in sales for the company.

Marina: Yes, that's right. It was a small company, so **I wore many hats**. It was very exciting.

Donna: What are you looking for in a job?

Marina: Well, I'm a real **people person**, so I would like a position where I have lots of *interaction* with different people.

Donna: Describe your ideal boss.

Marina: I work well with all different types of people. But I guess my ideal boss would be **hands-off**. I prefer to work independently and not to be **micro-managed.**

Donna: Tell me about a time when you had to **think outside the box** in your work.

Marina: When I was at Comtek, we didn't have any money to buy advertising. I **put in place** a program offering magazines a stand at the trade show in exchange for an advertisement in the magazine.

Donna: That sounds like a good idea! Tell me, what **sparked your interest** in our sales position?

Marina: I noticed from your job description that it requires a lot of interaction with the marketing department. I am very interested in marketing, so I thought this would be a good **stepping stone** to a marketing position.

Donna: Yes, this would be a good way to **get your foot in the door** of the marketing department.

IDIOMS & EXPRESSIONS – LESSON 28

between jobs – out of work; unemployed
быть незанятым; временно быть без работы

➤ Lucy is **between jobs** right now. She hopes to find a new job soon.

Примечание. Выражение "he is between jobs" (досл.: «между двух работ») звучит более мягко, чем "he is unemployed" («он безработный»).

(to) draw a blank – to be unable to remember
не в состоянии вспомнить что-либо; остаться ни с чем (досл.: вытянуть «пустой» лотерейный билет)

➤ I can't remember the name of the hotel where we stayed in Budapest. I'm **drawing a blank**.

(to) buy out – to purchase an entire business or someone's share of the business
выкупить весь бизнес или чью-либо долю в бизнесе; скупать акции

➤ When Richard's company was **bought out** by Microsoft, he was able to retire.

(to) let someone go – *see Lesson 27*

(to) wear many hats – to perform many different job responsibilities; to play many different roles
выполнять разнообразные должностные обязанности; совмещать несколько должностей; играть сразу несколько ролей

➤ There are only five employees at our company, so we all have to **wear many hats**.

people person – somebody who likes working with people; a friendly person
тот, кто любит работать с людьми; приветливый, дружелюбный человек

➤ You're sure to like Paul. He's a real **people person**.

hands-off – not too involved; passive; not interested in managing details
пассивный; безучастный; придерживающийся политики невмешательства

➤ Don't worry, Chris won't get involved in all of your projects. He's a **hands-off** manager.

(to) micro-manage – to manage too closely; to be too involved in the details; to not give an employee authority or freedom to make decisions
держать под строгим контролем; уделять чрезмерное внимание деталям; руководить по мелочам; лишать подчиненных инициативы

➤ Heidi gets involved in every detail of her employees' work. She has a reputation for **micro-managing**.

(to) think outside the box – *see Lesson 6*

(to) put in place – to establish; to start; to implement
учредить; стартовать; реализовать

> Next month, the company plans to **put in place** some new rules for filing expense reports.

(to) spark one's interest – to raise one's interest; to cause one to become interested in
вызвать, пробудить интерес; заинтересовать чем-либо; воодушевить

> An article in the *Wall Street Journal* **sparked Don's interest** in investing in Brazil.

stepping stone – a way of advancing or getting to the next stage; a position, a product, or an activity that comes first and prepares the way for what will come next
«трамплин»; средство для достижения цели; промежуточная ступень для дальнейшего продвижения

> Jennifer views her position as a human resource manager as a **stepping stone** to a larger position within her company.

(to) get one's foot in the door – to get into an organization; to get a position with an organization that could lead to a bigger opportunity in the future
сделать первый шаг, начать с чего-то; получить стартовую должность в компании с перспективой на дальнейший рост

> Taking a job as a receptionist is one way to **get your foot in the door** of a company.

☜ PRACTICE THE IDIOMS

Найдите наилучшую замену выделенным выражениям:

1) We received résumés from two candidates that **sparked our interest**. Please call them to arrange interviews.
   a) will definitely be hired
   b) aren't interesting
   c) look promising

2) I'm currently **between jobs**, but I'm confident I'll find something soon.
    a) on vacation
    b) employed
    c) unemployed

3) No wonder Carl is so good at sales. **He's a real people person.**
    a) He's good with people.
    b) He's good at his job.
    c) He doesn't like people.

4) Working at a small company with only four employees, Vijay is used to **wearing many hats**.
    a) working much too hard
    b) putting on a hat every morning
    c) doing many different things at work

5) Working as a summer intern is a good way to **get your foot in the door with a company**.
    a) get a full-time job at a company
    b) get promoted
    c) make money over the summer

6) Where does Wendy work? I know she told me, but **I'm drawing a blank**.
    a) I wasn't listening
    b) I can't remember
    c) I promised not to tell anybody

7) I suggest you take the sales analyst position. It's a **stepping stone to a better position**.
    a) way to get a better job in the future
    b) way to ensure you'll always be a sales analyst
    c) way to guarantee you'll be the sales director next year

8) Angela hardly ever sees her boss. **He's hands-off.**
    a) He keeps his hands off her.
    b) He doesn't manage her closely.
    c) He has his hands in everything.

ANSWERS TO LESSON 28, p. 195

I snapped up these chairs for a song.

JOB INTERVIEW 2

Sam currently runs his own company selling used office furniture online. He's tired of running his own business and wants to get a job with a big company.

Сэм управляет своей собственной компанией по продаже подержанной офисной мебели через Интернет. Он устал от руководства своим бизнесом и хочет попробовать получить работу в крупной корпорации.

Nick: I see from your résumé that you're **running your own show** as the owner of OldOfficeChair.com.

Sam: That's right. I've **carved out a niche** selling used office chairs over the Internet.

Nick: That sounds like a great business.

Sam: I was **making money hand over fist** after the *dot-com bust*. Companies were **going belly up** every day, and I **snapped up** all their chairs **for a song**. But these days it's becoming harder and harder to find used chairs.

Nick: Wouldn't you rather continue **working for yourself**?

Sam: No, I'm tired of working for myself.

Nick: I can **see the writing on the wall**: you'll **jump ship** when you think up another good business idea.

Sam: No, I won't. I'd always wanted to be an entrepreneur, but I **got that out of my system**. I realize now that **it's not all its cracked up to be**.

Nick: It certainly isn't. You work really hard and you're just as likely to **strike out** as you are to **strike it rich.**

Sam: **Tell me about it!** My best friend invested all his money in starting a company. He ended up **losing his shirt!**

Nick: Right, we all know people like that... One final point about the position. As you know, this is a large corporation. Are you sure you wouldn't be happier at a **start-up**?

Sam: **Start-ups** are exciting, but at this point in my life, I'm looking for stability over excitement. I've got four kids at home, and they like to eat!

Nick: I hear what you're saying. We could use somebody around here who thinks like an entrepreneur. If you're someone who can **take the ball and run with it**, you'd be a great addition.

IDIOMS & EXPRESSIONS – LESSON 29

(to) run one's own show – to run one's own business; to have control over an entire business or a part of a business
руководить своим собственным бизнесом; осуществлять контроль над всем бизнесом или его частью

➤ Anne can't imagine working for somebody else. She loves **running her own show** as CEO of Anne Global, Inc.

(to) carve out a niche – to start a specialty business
заполнить нишу; создать для себя нишу; начать узкоспециализированный бизнес

➤ Teresa **carved out a niche** selling DVDs on eBay.

Примечание. Имеется в виду определенный сегмент рынка.

(to) make money hand over fist – to make a lot of money; to make a lot of money fast
разбогатеть очень быстро, молниеносно, на глазах; урвать куш

➤ AstraZeneca **made money hand over fist** with the drug Prilosec. It was a huge success.

(to) go belly up – to go bankrupt
обанкротиться; выйти из бизнеса; разориться; лопнуть (о бизнесе)

➤ Shortly after Borders bookstore opened downtown, the small bookshop **went belly up**.

(to) snap up – to buy for a very good price; to buy a large supply of something, usually because it's on sale or in short supply
раскупать, расхватывать какой-либо товар по низкой цене; приобретать много товара, обычно с распродажи или если он в дефиците

➤ While in Vietnam, Monica **snapped up** dozens of inexpensive, beautiful silk scarves to sell at her Manhattan clothing boutique.

for a song – cheaply, inexpensively
очень дешево; за бесценок; почти даром

➤ Monica was able to buy clothing and accessories in Hanoi **for a song**.

(to) see the writing on the wall – to know what's coming; to see what's going to happen in the future
зловещее предзнаменование; предвидеть то, чему суждено случиться; чему быть – того не миновать

➤ The company has canceled this year's holiday party. I can **see the writing on the wall**: soon, they'll be announcing lay-offs.

Примечание. Встречается также вариант — see the handwriting on the wall.

Происхождение. Библейские письмена на стене. (Дан. 5-5, 28 о словах, написанных на стене во дворце Валтасара).

start-up – a small business, usually one that's been operating five years or less (and often in the technology industry)
небольшая вновь созданная компания (обычно не более 5 лет в бизнесе, часто в технологических отраслях); стартовый бизнес

➤ Julie took a chance by leaving her secure job at IBM to join a risky **start-up**.

(to) jump ship – to quit a job; to leave a job suddenly
«бежать с корабля»; оставить работу; поспешить уйти из компании

➤ When the accounting scandal broke, several financial managers at the energy company **jumped ship** immediately.

(to) get something out of one's system – to no longer feel the need to do something; to experience something to one's satisfaction
избавиться от какого-либо чувства, навязчивой идеи, потребности делать что-либо; получить полное удовлетворение

➤ Oleg had always wanted to be a lawyer, but after his summer internship at a law firm, he **got that out of his system**.

---

not all it's cracked up to be – not as great as people think; not as great as its reputation
все не так прекрасно, как кажется; не настолько хорошо, как об этом думают

➤ Working for a big public relations firm is **not all it's cracked up to be**. The pay isn't great and the hours are long.

(to) strike out – to fail
терпеть неудачу; выходить из игры

➤ I'm sorry to hear that you **struck out** on the job interview. I'm sure something else will come along soon.

Происхождение. Эта идиома пришла из бейсбола. Когда игрок три раза не попадает по мячу, он выходит из игры.

(to) strike it rich – to attain sudden financial success; to get rich quickly
добиться коммерческого успеха; неожиданно разбогатеть

➤ Richard **struck it rich** when Microsoft bought out his small software company.

Tell me about it! – I agree with you
Нельзя с вами не согласиться! Совершенно с вами согласен!

➤ "Our CEO really needs to get some new suits." — "**Tell me about it!** His suit is at least 25 years old!"

(to) lose one's shirt – to lose everything one owns; to lose a lot of money in business; to make a very bad investment

потерять последнюю рубашку; остаться без штанов; нести значительные финансовые убытки в бизнесе; неудачно вложить капитал

> It's risky to invest all of your money in the stock market. If the market goes down a lot, you could **lose your shirt**.

(to) take the ball and run with it – to take initiative; to take charge without a lot of supervision

взять инициативу в свои руки; взять на себя ответственность; работать самостоятельно; руководить проектом при минимальном контроле со стороны начальства

> We told the graphic designer what to include in the brochure, and she was able to **take the ball and run with it**.

✎ PRACTICE THE IDIOMS

Выберите наиболее подходящий ответ к каждому предложению:

1) We purchased an entire office building in New York for a song a few years ago when the economy was bad.
   a) Now that building would be much more expensive.
   b) Now that building would be much cheaper.
   c) Now you could probably get that building at a good price.

2) Kim, our new finance manager, is the type of person who can take the ball and run with it.
   a) Great, we need somebody here who needs a lot of direction.
   b) Great, we need some more good athletes in our office.
   c) Great, we're looking for somebody with initiative.

3) Jesse won $5 million last month in a lawsuit. He really struck it rich.
   a) No wonder he's decided to retire!
   b) No wonder he's decided to go to law school!
   c) No wonder he's decided to continue working!

4) We're looking to hire somebody who'll stay with our company for at least a few years. You wouldn't jump ship after just a year, would you?
   a) No, I don't even like sailing.
   b) No, I always stay at jobs at least three years.
   c) No, I would probably quit after a year.

5) You might get rich investing in biotech companies, but you're just as likely to lose your shirt.
   a) That's good advice. I'll definitely invest heavily in them.
   b) That's true. I'd better be careful about putting too much money into them.
   c) That's true, but I'd be willing to give away my shirt in ex change for a lot of money.

6) While in Russia, you should snap up some lacquer boxes. They're beautiful and inexpensive there.
   a) Okay, I will be sure to pack plenty of boxes.
   b) Okay, I will be sure to sell some lacquer boxes.
   c) Okay, I will be sure to buy some lacquer boxes.

7) I bought plane tickets on Econo-Airlines, and a few days later they went belly up!
   a) I'm sure you'll have a great flight.
   b) I'll be sure to book my next flight with Econo-Airlines.
   c) That's too bad. You'd better buy some new plane tickets.

8) Working on Wall Street for an investment bank sounds wonderful, but it's not all it's cracked up to be.
   a) You're right. It really is wonderful.
   b) You're right. The pay is good, but the work is demanding and the hours are long.
   c) You're right. Everybody I know who works on Wall Street loves it.

ANSWERS TO LESSON 29, p. 195

NEGOTIATING A SALARY OFFER
Part 1

Donna calls Marina to tell her the good news — she got the job. Marina wisely decides to negotiate for a higher salary.

Донна звонит Марине, чтобы сообщить ей приятную новость: ее берут на работу. Марина принимает мудрое решение: попробовать сразу договориться о более высокой зарплате.

Donna: Marina, it's Donna Harris from American Steel Enterprises. I've got great news. We'd like to make you an offer.

Marina: That's fantastic!

Donna: Our HR department will go over the **nitty-gritty** of the offer with you, but let me give you **the big picture** now. The *base salary* will be $45,000.

Marina: I'm really excited about this opportunity. I should mention that I'm **weighing another offer** with a higher *base salary*. **Is there any room to negotiate**?

Donna: What did you **have in mind**?

Marina: Well, my other offer is for $50,000. Can you match it?

Donna: That's **out of our range**. Let's **split the difference**. We'll go up to $47,500.

Marina: Can we say $48,000?

Donna: No, I'm afraid not. Our final offer is $47,500.

Marina: This sounds good, but I'd like to **sleep on it**. Can I call you back tomorrow?

Donna: Yes, but please **touch base with** me **first thing in the morning** so we can **get the ball rolling**. We've got several other candidates interested in the position.

Part 2: The Next Day

Marina: Donna, I've had a chance to **review your offer**. I'm going to **stand my ground**. To accept your offer, I really need $48,000.

Donna: Marina, you **drive a hard bargain**! But, okay, I think that can be arranged. Can you start on Monday, 9 a.m.?

Marina: That'll be perfect. See you then!

IDIOMS & EXPRESSIONS – LESSON 30

nitty-gritty – the details
детали; подробности какого-то дела; повседневная работа

> I don't need to know the **nitty-gritty** of what happened during your meeting with the client. Just tell me the main points.

Примечание. Точные корни этого выражения неизвестны. По одной из версий, оно относится к категории забавных выражений, построенных на игре повторяющихся сходных звуков, подобно таким выражениям, как "wishy-washy" (см. гл. 8), "itsy-bitsy" («крохотный, малюсенький»), "mish-mash" («странное сочетание», «неожиданная комбинация вещей»).

the big picture – a summary; an overview; the most important points
итог; обзор; наиболее важные моменты; общая картина

> Let me start off this presentation by giving you **the big picture** of what's happening now in our industry.

SYNONYM: 10,000-foot view. Example: Do you want to know the details, or should I just give you the **10,000-foot view** of the problem?

(to) weigh another offer – to consider another offer, usually a job offer

взвесить альтернативное предложение; рассмотреть другое предложение (обычно по трудоустройству)

➤ Brian told Pfizer he was **weighing another offer** and that he would give them an answer next week.

Is there any room to negotiate? – Is it possible to negotiate? Are you flexible about the offer?

Есть ли возможность для обсуждения этого предложения? Насколько гибко вы готовы обсуждать условия?

➤ Your offer is a little lower than I had hoped for. **Is there any room to negotiate?**

(to) have in mind – to be thinking of

думать о чем-либо; держать что-либо на уме; иметь в виду

➤ Kyle said he wanted to go somewhere exotic for this year's company offsite. Do you know where he **had in mind**?

---

out of one's range – more than one wants to pay

сверх установленного лимита; больше, чем хотелось бы заплатить; не в чьей-либо компетенции

➤ PlastiCase Industries tried to sell us the cases for five dollars each, but we told them that was **out of our range**.

(to) split the difference – to accept a figure halfway in between; to compromise

согласиться разделить издержки поровну; идти на компромисс

➤ You're asking for $500 for this used office chair, but we only budgeted $300 for it. Let's **split the difference** and say $400.

(to) sleep on it – to think about a decision overnight; to take a day to decide on something

тщательно обдумать предложение; взять время на обдумывание; утро вечера мудренее

➤ Thanks for your offer, but I'm not sure I want to move from the marketing department to the sales department. Let me **sleep on it**.

(to) touch base with – *see Lesson 3*

first thing in the morning – early in the morning
первым делом; то, что надо сделать в первую очередь в начале рабочего дня

> If the report isn't ready by the time you leave this evening, please have it on my desk **first thing in the morning**.

(to) get the ball rolling – to get started
запустить в работу; начать или продолжить что-либо

> If the toy company wants to have their new line of mini-robots out by the holiday season, they'd better **get the ball rolling** now.

(to) review an offer – to think about an offer; to consider an offer
рассмотреть, взвесить, обдумать предложение

> After **reviewing your offer** carefully, I've decided to take a job with another company.

(to) stand one's ground – to maintain and defend one's position; to refuse to give up one's position
твердо стоять на своем; отстаивать свое мнение; не сдавать своих позиций

> Earthy Foods wanted to open a large grocery store in the historic downtown area, but the small town **stood its ground** and refused to let them build there.

(to) drive a hard bargain – to be tough in negotiating an agreement; to negotiate something in one's favor
много запрашивать, не соглашаться на меньшее; жестко обсуждать условия договора; вести жесткие переговоры в чью-либо пользу

> We don't usually offer such a big discount on our products, but you **drove a hard bargain**.

✎ PRACTICE THE IDIOMS

Заполните пропуски, используя следующие идиомы:

out of our range	first thing in the morning
split the difference	weighing another offer
room to negotiate	drive a hard bargain
big picture	review our offer

Karen: Hi, it's Karen Chen from Citigroup calling to see if you've had a chance to _____(1)_____.

Rick: Hi, Karen. I still haven't made up my mind. I'm _____(2)_____ from another financial services company.

Karen: Oh really? What are they offering? Just tell me the _____(3)_____. I don't need to know the details.

Rick: They're offering a base salary of $80,000, plus bonus.

Karen: Oh, goodness. I'm afraid $80,000 is _____(4)_____.

Rick: Well, I'm still very interested in Citigroup. Is there any _____(5)_____?

Karen: Our offer to you was for $65,000. We can _____(6)_____ and offer you $72,000.

Rick: Your offer would be more attractive at $75,000 with a guaranteed bonus of $7,500.

Karen: You _____(7)_____! Let me talk to our senior management. I'll get back to you tomorrow, _____(8)_____.

ANSWERS TO LESSON 30, p. 195

Вставьте пропущенные слова:

1) We've discussed this issue long enough. Let's just cut ____ the chase and make a decision.

   a) at   b) up   c) to

2) If you want to get your ____ in the door of an advertising agency, you should try to get an internship.

   a) body   b) foot   c) leg

3) This past quarter you sold over $1 million worth of insurance policies. Keep ____ the good work!

   a) at   b) with   c) up

4) Companies are making money hand ____ fist selling music downloads over the Internet.

   a) over   b) above   c) upon

5) Right now Rachel doesn't want to take an international assignment. However, she might consider working in China down the ____.

   a) lane   b) street   c) road

6) Emily was sure that her analysis was correct, so she stood her ____ when others criticized it.

   a) field   b) opinion   c) ground

7) You're selling color photo printers for only $39? People are sure to snap those ____!

   a) down   b) through   c) up

184

8) Tanya gets bored doing the same thing all day. She's looking for a job where she's required to _____ many hats.

    a) wear   b) sew   c) make

9) Troy decided to retire after General Mills bought _____ his small organic food company.

    a) up   b) out   c) in

10) Debra took a job as a marketing assistant, hoping it would be a stepping _____ to a management position in the future.

    a) point   b) stone   c) rock

11) You don't have to give Frank a lot of detailed direction. He knows how to take the ball and _____ with it.

    a) run   b) walk   c) jump

12) We'd be interested in renting this office space from you if you can lower the price. Four thousand dollars per month is simply _____ our range.

    a) within   b) into   c) out of

13) Martin was laid off from his job six months ago, and he still hasn't found a new position. He's _____ jobs.

    a) among   b) between   c) out of

14) These days, you can register domain names on the Internet _____ a song.

    a) in   b) for   c) with

15) If you're having trouble reaching a decision, why don't you sleep _____ it and give your answer tomorrow.

    a) with   b) over   c) on

ANSWERS TO REVIEW, p. 195

bells and whistles the name of the game track record the best of both worlds on top of trends through the roof on the same page noth... ...d pull out all the stops ... ...ze at a pat on the back cash cow step up to the plate dream up on the right track

ad campaign – краткая форма от «advertising campaign», рекламная кампания. Разработка серии рекламных объявлений для размещения в средствах массовой информации (таких как радио, телевидение, Интернет) в целях продвижения на рынке определенного продукта или линии продукции.

agenda item – пункт повестки – одна из тем повестки дня, которые предстоит обсудить на совещании

analytical – аналитический – относящий к анализу и способности логически решать те или иные проблемы

(to) associate a brand with – ассоциировать брэнд с чем-то позитивным, мысленно связывать с чем-либо торговую марку фирмы

base salary – базовая зарплата – зарплата без учета бонусов и других льгот

brand equity – ценность торговой марки – совокупность активов компании, связанных с торговой маркой (напр., дополнительным активом для компании является тот факт, что высоко оцененная потребителями торговая марка стимулирует рост продаж как уже известных потребителю товаров, так и новых товаров, которые будут выпускаться под той же маркой)

CFO – краткая форма от «chief financial officer», главный финансовый директор. Один из руководителей компании, отвечающий за финансовые вопросы.

company offsite – выездное мероприятие, во время которого работники компании собираются вместе вне офиса, для того чтобы развлечься и обсудить перспективы фирмы на будущее

corner office – угловой офис – наиболее престижный кабинет в компании, обычно предназначенный для высокого руководства

differentiated products – дифференцированные товары – продукция с отличительными качественными характеристиками или особыми свойствами, которые выделяют их на фоне конкурентных товаров

186

dot-com bust – провал интернет-компаний – период 2000-2002 гг., когда многие интернет-компании вышли из бизнеса, обанкротились

(to) double-check – двойная проверка – перепроверять, проверять несколько раз, сверять

downsize – сокращать штат сотрудников, увольнять часть персонала

endorsement – поддержка; подтверждение; одобрение

ergonomic – эргономические товары – товары, дизайн которых максимально учитывает особенности человеческого тела , что делает их очень комфортабельными и удобными в использовании

figure – денежные суммы (в цифрах, например, $4500)

focus groups – фокус-группы – один из способов изучения рынка, при котором проводится опрос небольшой группы людей для выявления их мнения о товарах или услугах. Фокус-группы часто используются для изучения спроса на новые товары или при подготовке рекламных кампаний

forecast – прогнозирование – приблизительная подсчет, оценка; прогнозирование перспективного спроса на товары и услуги

franching – франчайзинг – специальный вид лицензирования, когда компания, владеющая известной торговой маркой, предоставляет другим фирмам привилегию ставить эту торговую марку на свою продукцию, при этом оставляя за собой право контролировать качество продукции, производимой компанией-франчайзером

freebie – что-либо, полученное бесплатно, даром, обычно в качестве рекламных сувениров

fruit smoothie – напиток, приготовленный с помощью блендера. В его состав входят фруктовый сок, цельный фрукт, лед и иногда йогурт

grand – штука баксов (разг.); тысяча долларов – в этом значении употребляется в основном в разговорной речи

innovative – новаторский – совершенно новый; оригинальный; передовой

inventory – инвентарь, опись, список, реестр – товары, которые еще не проданы, а также сырье (детали для сборки)

launch – запускать – имеет несколько значений, но в данной ситуации означает: «выпустить на рынок». Другие значения: (1) начать новую карьеру; (2) запускать, приводить в движение (ракету)

launch a website – запустить вэб-сайт – разместить новый вэб-сайт на Интернете

low carb – краткая форма от "low carbohydrate"– низкое содержание углеводов. Низкоуглеводная диета, предложенная доктором Аткинсом, завоевала широкую популярность в 2002 году. Многие компании-производители пищевых продуктов и напитков стали специализироваться на низкоуглеводных продуктах и получили большие прибыли, сыграв на популярности этой диеты.

market demand – рыночный спрос – общий спрос на товары и услуги

mascot – талисман – символ компании или спортивной команды, приносящий удачу

optional – необязательный, факультативный

overtime pay – сверхурочные – почасовая оплата за отработанное сверх нормы время, обычно оплачивается в полуторном или двойном размере

overview – обзор (деятельности)

P & L – краткая форма от «profit & loss». В обязанности ответственных за "profit & loss" входит обеспечение прибыльности бизнеса. Они составляют "P & L statement" – сводный финансовый отчет, или отчет о прибыли.

perks – краткая форма от «perquisites» – льготы помимо зарплаты, приработок, чаевые

price quote – расценки, договорная цена; квота

private-label products – товар под частной маркой – выпускается одной компанией, а продается под торговой маркой продавца; товар, изготовленный специально для определенного магазина и пущенный в продажу с этикеткой этого магазина

product life cycles – жизненный цикл продукта – стадии, которые проходит продукт с момента запуска на рынок. Эти стадии включают: представление, рост, полная зрелость и спад. Маркетинговая стратегия базируется на том, на какой стадии жизненного цикла пребывает продукт в данный момент.

product line – линия товаров – группа схожих товаров; ассортимент товаров, предлагаемых на рынок одним и тем же производителем

pros and cons – за и против – положительные и отрицательные стороны

prototype – прототип – опытный образец новой продукции, модель, обычно используемая для разработки дизайна и усовершенствования технологии до момента запуска в производство законченного продукта

R&D – краткая форма от «research & development». Отдел исследований и разработок в компании, который выдвигает идеи производства новой улучшенной продукции и усовершенствования процессов производства, а также проводит проверку продуктов на качество.

rag – одно из значений: низкопробная газетенка, заполненная объявлениями и плохо написанными статьями

reference – рекомендация, предоставляемая работодателю потенциальным сотрудником с бывшего места работы относительно его квалификации и характера

relic – реликт, архаизм – несовременный, устаревший, пережиток прошлого; буквально: реликвии, мощи, предметы религиозного поклонения, как например, мощи святого

salary freeze – замораживание заработной платы – временная приостановка роста зарплаты, связанная с финансовыми трудностями

severance package – выходное пособие – льготы, предоставляемые служащим, которые были уволены в связи с сокращением штата

sexual harassment – сексуальные домогательства – непоощряемый словесный или физический контакт сексуального характера, который имеет непосредственное влияние на продвижение по службе и создает неприятную атмосферу на работе

shopping cart – корзина для покупок – корзина или тележка для покупок в продуктовых магазинах, а так же в виртуальных магазинах на вэб-сайтах

short by – недостающая продукция; нехватка товаров

soles – подошвы, подметки у обуви

strip joint – стриптиз-клуб – бар, в котором женщины раздеваются на сцене для развлечения мужской клиентуры

summer intern – летний интерн (практикант) – студент или недавний выпускник вуза, проходящий производственную практику в компании в летнее время для получения практического опыта

tough – трудный, сложный

bells and whistles the name of the game track record the best
of both worlds on top of trends through the roof on the same
page noth... КЛЮЧИ К УПРАЖНЕНИЯМ ...pull out
all the stops in a n... ...at a pat on the
back cash cow step up to the plate dream up on the right track

LESSON 1: TALKING ABOUT A NEW PROJECT

1. b	5. c
2. a	6. c
3. b	7. a
4. a	8. b

LESSON 2: TALKING ABOUT FINANCIAL ISSUES

1. a	5. a
2. b	6. a
3. c	7. c
4. b	8. b

LESSON 3: TALKING ABOUT A NEW AD CAMPAIGN

1. b	5. c
2. a	6. a
3. a	7. c
4. b	8. b

LESSON 4: TALKING ABOUT MANUFACTURING

1. 24/7	5. working down to the wire
2. does whatever it takes	6. cutting it close
3. work out the kinks	7. reality check
4. fine-tuning	8. get the job done

LESSON 5: TALKING ABOUT COMPANY STRATEGY

1. b	5. a
2. c	6. b
3. b	7. c
4. b	8. c

REVIEW: LESSONS 1-5

1. b	4. c	7. c	10. b	13. c
2. a	5. c	8. b	11. c	14. b
3. a	6. a	9. a	12. b	15. a

LESSON 6: DISCUSSING GOOD RESULTS

1. b	5. c
2. c	6. a
3. a	7. b
4. a	8. b

LESSON 7: DISCUSSING BAD RESULTS

1. running in place
2. eating their lunch
3. no wonder
4. on top of trends
5. bring some new products to market
6. in deep trouble
7. face the music
8. new blood

LESSON 8: DISCUSSING A DIFFICULT DECISION

1. b	5. c
2. c	6. b
3. b	7. a
4. a	8. b

LESSON 9: DEALING WITH A DISSATISFIED CUSTOMER

1. deliver
2. Where to begin
3. a far cry from
4. mince words
5. pulled out all the stops
6. pull the wool over my eyes
7. pretty penny
8. make it up to you

LESSON 10: DISCUSSING A DIFFICULT REQUEST

1. c	5. c
2. a	6. b
3. a	7. a
4. b	8. c

REVIEW: LESSONS 6-10

1. b	4. a	7. a	10. a	13. b
2. c	5. c	8. c	11. b	14. c
3. c	6. b	9. a	12. b	15. b

LESSON 11: MOTIVATING CO-WORKERS

1. turn around our business
2. throw in the towel
3. count me in
4. on board
5. rally the troops
6. team spirit
7. working their tails off
8. track record

LESSON 12: RUNNING A MEETING

1. b	5. a
2. c	6. c
3. b	7. c
4. a	8. b

LESSON 13: DISCUSSING A MISTAKE

1. I could've sworn that
2. drop the ball
3. asleep at the wheel
4. blow things out of proportion
5. no big deal
6. dot your i's and cross your t's
7. up to scratch
8. bitter pill to swallow

LESSON 14: TAKING CREDIT FOR GOOD RESULTS

1. a	5. b
2. b	6. a
3. c	7. a
4. b	8. c

LESSON 15: SHIFTING BLAME

1. c	5. c
2. b	6. a
3. b	7. c
4. a	8. a

REVIEW: LESSONS 11-15

1. c	4. a	7. b	10. c	13. a
2. b	5. c	8. a	11. a	14. c
3. c	6. b	9. a	12. b	15. c

LESSON 16: POLITELY DISAGREEING WITH SOMEONE

1. c	5. a
2. a	6. c
3. b	7. a
4. b	8. c

LESSON 17: TELLING SOMEBODY OFF

1. pulling his weight
2. sick and tired
3. the last straw
4. shape up or ship out
5. What's the deal?
6. slave driver
7. run a tight ship
8. turn a blind eye
9. cut me some slack
10. spare me the sob story

LESSON 18: DISCUSSING OFFICE SCANDALS

1. c	5. b
2. b	6. b
3. a	7. a
4. b	8. c

LESSON 19: COMPLAINING ABOUT A CO-WORKER

1. hot-head
2. steer clear
3. issues with her
4. gets under his skin
5. grin and bear it
6. in a snit
7. get bent out of shape
8. push my buttons

LESSON 20: TALKING ABOUT A BROWN NOSER

1. a	5. b
2. c	6. a
3. c	7. c
4. b	8. b

REVIEW: LESSONS 16-20

1. b	4. c	7. a	10. b	13. c
2. a	5. b	8. c	11. a	14. b
3. c	6. b	9. a	12. c	15. b

LESSON 21: EXPLAINING THAT YOU'RE FEELING OVERWORKED

1. a	5. c
2. c	6. b
3. b	7. b
4. a	8. a

LESSON 22: CALLING IN SICK

1. under the weather
2. killing me
3. call in sick
4. up to my ears in work
5. I'm not feeling so hot
6. there's something going around
7. take it easy
8. in tip-top shape

LESSON 23: REQUESTING A BANK LOAN

1. b	5. c
2. a	6. a
3. b	7. c
4. b	8. c

LESSON 24: NEGOTIATING A PURCHASE

1. more bang for the buck
2. break my budget
3. the hard sell
4. at no extra charge
5. no can do
6. nickel-and-dime
7. on a tight budget
8. it's a deal

LESSON 25: CONDUCTING A PERFORMANCE REVIEW

1. b	5. c
2. b	6. a
3. c	7. a
4. a	8. b

Review: Lessons 21-25

1. c	4. a	7. c	10. c	13. b
2. b	5. b	8. b	11. a	14. a
3. b	6. a	9. b	12. c	15. b

Lesson 26: Promoting an Employee

1. c	5. c
2. b	6. b
3. a	7. b
4. c	8. c

Lesson 27: Firing Somebody

1. reduce headcount
2. let them go
3. work has really slipped
4. lifted a finger
5. take credit for
6. build the company from the ground up
7. at the top of her game
8. burned out
9. her hands are tied
10. no hard feelings

Lesson 28: Job Interview 1

1. c	5. a
2. c	6. b
3. a	7. a
4. c	8. b

Lesson 29: Job Interview 2

1. a	5. b
2. c	6. c
3. a	7. c
4. b	8. b

Lesson 30: Negotiating a Salary Offer

1. review our offer
2. weighing another offer
3. big picture
4. out of our range
5. room to negotiate
6. split the difference
7. drive a hard bargain
8. first thing in the morning

Review: Lessons 26-30

1. c	4. a	7. c	10. b	13. b
2. b	5. c	8. a	11. a	14. b
3. c	6. c	9. b	12. c	15. c

A

"A" player, 156
according to the rumor mill, 108
all in a day's work, 84
arm and a leg, an 18
around the clock, 83
as sick as a dog, 134
asleep at the wheel, 79
at a premium, 30
at no extra charge, 145
at one's expense, 119
at the end of the day, 24
at the top of one's game, 162

B

back and forth on an issue, 48
back-of-the-envelope calculations, 10
bat around some ideas, 98
beef up, 30
bells and whistles, 4
belt-tightening, 97
bent out of shape, 114
best of both worlds, the, 49
between a rock and a hard place, 97
between jobs, 168
beyond the call of duty, 151
big picture, the, 180
big win, 5
bigwig, 60
bite the bullet, 48
bitter pill to swallow, 79
blockbuster, 4
blow things out of proportion, 78
blows my mind, 11
bottom line, 96
brainstorm, 16
break even, 12

break one's budget, 144
break the news, 157
bring a product to market, 44
brown noser, 118
brownie points, 118
build from the ground up, 163
burn one's bridges, 105
burn the midnight oil, 82
burned out, 162
butter up, 119
buy out, 169

C

call in sick, 134
call it quits, 66
can-do attitude, 59
can't afford to, 135
carve out a niche, 174
cash cow, 29
cash in on, 44
child's play, 60
Chill out!, 121
circle back to, 74
clean house, 44
climb the corporate ladder, 120
come up with a winner, 4
come with the territory, 84
compare apples to oranges, 139
count me in, 68
cover a lot of ground, 72
cover oneself, 88
crunch the numbers, 11
crunch time, 128
cut back on, 96
cut it a little close, 23
cut someone some slack, 103
cut to the chase, 163
cutting-edge, 28

D

deliver, 54
different animal, 139
do a 180, 150
do whatever it takes, 24
dog-eat-dog world, 119
don't push your luck, 158
don't waste your breath, 104
dot your i's and cross your t's, 78
down the road, 158
draw a blank, 168
Dream on!, 90
dream up, 37
drive a hard bargain, 182
drop the ball, 79
drum up business, 37
dump someone, 102

E

earn one's keep, 156
eating one's lunch, 43
educated guess, 10
80/20 rule, 130
every time I turn around, 73

F

face the music, 42
fall guy, 88
far cry from, a, 54
fast followers, 28
fast track a project, 4
fine-tune, 22
first thing in the morning, 182
flesh out something, 19
for a song, 175
for starters, 30
for the record, 23

G

game plan, 6
generate lots of buzz, 17
get ahead, 120
get buy-in, 30
get down to business, 68

get nailed, 109
get off track, 73
get one's foot in the door, 170
get right on something, 55
get something off the ground, 6
get something out of one's system, 176
get the ball rolling, 182
get the job done, 24
get to the bottom of something, 43
get under one's skin, 115
get up to speed, 150
get wind of, 5
get with the program, 29
give it one's best shot, 59
give somebody an earful, 114
give somebody the green light, 12
give one a run for one's money, 38
go all out, 54
go back to the drawing board, 139
go belly up, 175
go-getter, 157
go on about, 89
go the extra mile, 157
good call, 49
grin and bear it, 115
guerrilla marketing, 36

H

half-baked idea, 17
hands-off, 169
hang in there, 129
happy medium, 146
hard sell, the, 144
have a chip on one's shoulder, 115
have a knack for something, 150
have a lot on one's plate, 129
have a rough night, 102
have in mind, 181
have some issues, 115
head is on the chopping block, one's, 12
he'll get his, 110
hit the ground running, 156
hot-head, 114
hunker down, 83

I

I beg to differ, 73
I can't believe my ears!, 88
I could've sworn that, 78
I don't know whether I'm coming or going, 128
I wasn't born yesterday!, 121
icing on the cake, 18
in a nutshell, 72
in a snit, 114
in deep trouble, 42
in hot water, 11
in the bag, 139
in the red, 11
in tip-top shape, 135
Is there any room to negotiate?, 181
issue at hand, the, 74
it's a deal, 146

J

jump ship, 176
jump the gun, 72
jump through hoops, 140
just for the record, 23

K

keep an open mind, 16
keep one's eye on the prize, 83
keep one's head above water, 129
keep one's nose to the grindstone, 130
keep someone in the loop, 150
keep something under wraps, 5
Keep up the good work!, 158
kick off, 58
kiss up to someone, 118
know something inside and out, 138
kudos to, 36

L

last resort, 97
last straw, the, 105
latest dirt, the, 108
leapfrog one's competitors, 29
leaving us, 157

lesser of two evils, the, 97
let someone go, 163
let's just agree to disagree, 98
likely story, 121
live to regret a decision, 49
look at oneself in the mirror, 120
lose one's shirt, 177

M

make a killing, 5
make a mountain out of a molehill, 78
make a pass at someone, 108
make a splash, 144
make it up to you, 55
make money hand over fist, 174
make the grade, 157
market share, 42
me-too products, 29
mess around, 55
micro-manage, 169
mince words, 54
miss the point, 140
more bang for the buck, 145
move on, 74
mum's the word, 5
my gut tells me, 49
my hands are tied, 164
my stomach is killing me, 134

N

name of the game, the, 97
need like a hole in the head, 58
new blood, 44
nickel-and-dime, 146
nitty-gritty, 180
no big deal, 78
no-brainer, 139
no can do, 145
no hard feelings, 164
no ifs, ands, or buts, 22
no wonder, 42
not a bad guy, 114
not able to make heads or tails of, 151
not all it's cracked up to be, 176

not feel so hot, 134
not lift a finger, 163
not see eye-to-eye, 73
not so hot, 150
nothing is set in stone, 16
nothing to sneeze at, 138
nothing ventured, nothing gained, 59

O

of two minds, 48
off the record, 146
on a tight budget, 145
on board, 68
on one's high horse, 115
on the dot, 103
on the make, 108
on the right track, 17
on the same page, 30
on top of trends, 43
opportunity areas, 151
out for oneself, 119
out of hand, 73
out of one's mind, 58
out of one's range, 181
out of the loop, 108
out of the question, 97
out of touch with reality, 60

P

pan out, 37
pass the buck, 89
pat on the back, a, 36
people person, 169
pitch in, 83
play one's cards right, 158
plug a product, 18
point fingers at each other, 90
politically correct (PC), 109
pretty penny, 54
pride oneself on, 151
pull one's weight, 102
pull out all the stops, 54
pull something off, 82
pull the plug, 12

pull the wool over one's eyes, 55
push one's buttons, 114
push one's luck, 158
push the envelope, 82
put a stake in the ground, 49
put in one's two cents, 74
put in place, 170
put one's mind to something, 59

R

R&R, 84
rally the troops, 68
read between the lines, 163
real dog, 29
reality check, 23
record-breaking, 36
reduce headcount, 164
rest on one's laurels, 67
review an offer, 182
rip off, 6
roll up one's sleeves, 59
run a tight ship, 103
run in place, 44
run numbers, 11
run one's own show, 174
run some ideas by, 16
run with an idea, 18
running behind, 104

S

save a bundle, 96
scale back one's hours, 129
see the writing on the wall, 175
settle down, 129
Shape up or ship out!, 103
share the credit, 38
shell out, 88
sick and tired of, 102
sign on new customers, 37
slave driver, 105
sleep on it, 181
slip one's mind, 128
snap up, 175
spare us the sob story, 102

spark one's interest, 170
split the difference, 181
stand firm, 146
stand one's ground, 182
start-up, 175
steer clear of, 114
step up to the plate, 23
stepping stone, 170
stocking stuffer, 4
stressed out, 128
strike gold, 89
strike it rich, 176
strike out, 176
swamped, 55

T

tagline, 19
take a crack at something, 58
take credit for something, 162
take it easy, 135
take it from there, 151
take someone into one's confidence, 157
take the ball and run with it, 177
take the cake, 109
talk about, 119
talk behind someone's back, 121
talk someone into something, 88
team player, 83
team spirit, 68
Tell me about it!, 176
test the waters, 49
that's putting it lightly, 73
there's something going around, 135
think outside the box, 37
think twice, 121
through the roof, 36
throw cold water over, 17
throw in the towel, 66
throw something in, 145
to the tune of, 42
touch base with, 19
tough call, 48

track something down, 90
track record, 67
turn a blind eye to something, 103
turn around one's business, 67
24-7, 24
twist somebody's arm, 18

U

un-PC, 109
under one's belt, 138
under the weather, 134
until one is blue in the face, 98
up to one's ears in work, 135
up to one's old tricks, 108
up to scratch, 79

W

walls have ears, the, 121
wash one's hands of, 89
We've been down before, but we
    always come back fighting, 67
wear many hats, 169
weigh another offer, 181
weigh in on, 73
what goes around comes around, 110
What's the deal?, 102
What's up?, 134
when push comes to shove, 164
Where to begin?, 55
Why mess with success?, 28
wiped out, 129
wishy-washy, 48
work down to the wire, 24
work has slipped, one's, 162
work one's tail off, 66
work out the kinks, 22

Y

yes man, 118
You took the words right out of my
    mouth!, 44

Об авторе

Эмми Жиллетт преподавала английский язык как иностранный в Стэмфорде (штат Коннектикут, США) и в Праге (Чешская Республика). Ее заметки и юмористические рассказы были опубликованы во многих печатных изданиях, таких как *MAD Magazine*, *San Francisco Chronicle* и *Family Circle*. Эмми является автором бестселлера «Говорите по-английски как американцы», который с успехом распространяется в 10 странах мира.

Лексические обороты для этой книги постепенно отбирались автором на протяжении долгих лет плодотворной деловой карьеры в таких организациях как Hewlett-Packard, Госдепартамент США, Мичиганский университет.

Эмми — выпускница Стэнфордского университета со специализацией в славянских языках и литературе. Она имеет степень магистра русского языка и славянской филологии, а также ученую степень от Корнельского университета. Кроме того, Эмми совершенствовала знание русского языка в Санкт-Петербургском Государственном университете (Россия).

О переводчике

Лариса Кесельман, профессиональный переводчик и преподаватель. Родилась в Москве. Выпускница Московского Государственного института иностранных языков им. Мориса Тореза, ныне Государственный лингвистический университет. Владеет русским, английским, французским и испанским языками. В течение многих лет работала переводчиком и менеджером по переводам в американской выставочной фирме «Комтек», переводя на русский язык и редактируя журнал «Бизнес и выставки» и официальные каталоги выставок.

Please visit our website, where you'll find:

- Additional practice exercises for **Speak Business English Like an American**
- Interesting links for studying English
- More books from Language Success Press

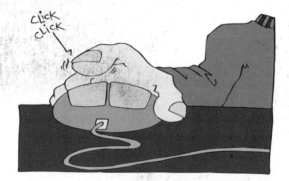

www.languagesuccesspress.com

LANGUAGE SUCCESS PRESS

ORDER FORM

TITLE	Quantity	Line Total
Lose Your Accent in 28 Days™ (Complete System with Workbook, CD-ROM, Audio CD)...$49.95		
Speak Business English Like an American for Native Russian Speakers (Book & Audio CD)...$29.95		
Speak Business English Like an American for Speakers of Any Language (Book & Audio CD)...$29.95		
Speak English Like an American® for Native Russian Speakers (Book & Audio CD)...$24.95		
Speak English Like an American® for Speakers of Any Language (Book & Audio CD)...$24.95		
Subtotal		
Shipment to Michigan Add 6% Sales Tax		
Shipping (see below)		
TOTAL		

U.S. Shipping: $4.95 for orders up to $50. $6.95 for orders from $50.01 to $75. $8.95 for orders $75.01-$100. $11.95 for orders from $100.01-$200. Add an additional $4 for each additional $100 or part thereof. **International Shipping**: Canada & Mexico: Multiply the U.S. shipping rate by 1.5. Overseas Shipping: Multiply the U.S. shipping rate by 2.

Please charge my: ❑ VISA ❑ MASTERCARD ❑ AMERICAN EXPRESS

Card #_____Expiration_____

Name on card_____

Ship to:

Name_____

Organization_____

Address_____

City_____ State_____ Zip_____ Country_____

Phone_____ E-mail_____

▤ FAX this form to Language Success Press: 1-303-484-2004

✆ ORDER ONLINE: www.languagesuccesspress.com